The National Audubon Society

SPEAKING FOR NATURE

A CENTURY OF CONSERVATION

The National Audubon Society

SPEAKING FOR NATURE

A CENTURY OF CONSERVATION

Edited by Les Line

Hugh Lauter Levin Associates, Inc.

Published by Hugh Lauter Levin Associates, Inc.

Sidebar excerpts courtesy of the authors and *Audubon* magazine from its December 1998 issue.

Editor: Les Line
Design: Lori S. Malkin
Photo Research: Niki Barrie
Project Editor: James O. Muschett
Director of Audubon Books: Katherine R. Santone

Photo credits:
PAGE 1: Great egret. (Photo: John Shaw)
PAGES 2-3: Flock of terns and gulls in flight. (Photo: Mitsuaki Iwago/Minden Pictures)
PAGES 4-5: Bull elk, Yellowstone National Park. (Photo: Daniel J. Cox/Natural Exposures)
TITLE PAGE: Great blue heron and young. (Photo: Art Morris/Birds As Art)
OPPOSITE: Layson albatross, Hawaii. (Photo: Daniel J. Cox/Natural Exposures)
CONTENTS: Brown bears salmon fishing, Alaska. (Photo: Natalie B. Fobes)
PAGE 13: Arctic tern. (Photo: Thomas D. Mangelsen)

ISBN 0-88363-799-5
Printed in Hong Kong
Distributed by Publishers Group West

OUR MISSION

The mission of NATIONAL AUDUBON SOCIETY is to conserve and restore natural ecosystems, focusing on birds, other wildlife, and their habitats for the benefit of humanity and the earth's biological diversity.

One of the largest, most effective environmental organizations, AUDUBON has 550,000 members, 100 sanctuaries, state offices, and nature centers, and 500+ chapters in the Americas, plus a professional staff of scientists, lobbyists, lawyers, policy analysts, and educators.

The award-winning *Audubon* magazine, published six times a year and sent to all members, carries outstanding articles and color photography on wildlife and nature, presenting in-depth reports on critical environmental issues, as well as conservation news and commentary. AUDUBON also publishes *Audubon Adventures,* a children's nature newspaper reaching 450,000 students in grades 4-6. Through ecology camps and workshops in Maine, Connecticut, and Wyoming, AUDUBON offers professional development for educators and activists; through *Audubon Expedition Institute* in Belfast, Maine, the Society offers unique, traveling undergraduate and graduate degree programs in Environmental Education.

NATIONAL AUDUBON SOCIETY also sponsors books, field guides, and CD ROM programs, plus nature travel to exotic places like Africa, Antarctica, Baja California, Patagonia, and the Galapagos Islands.

For information about how to become an AUDUBON member, subscribe to *Audubon Adventures,* or learn more about our camps and workshops, please write or call:

NATIONAL AUDUBON SOCIETY
Membership Dept.
700 Broadway
New York, New York 10003
(800) 274-4201 or (212) 979-3000
http://www.audubon.org/

CONTENTS

FOREWORD

IF THERE IS ONE LESSON that the history of conservation teaches, it is that the greatest victories were not won by powerful special interests, but by grassroots efforts. It has been said that all politics is local. By extension, all effective conservation has the roots of its success firmly planted in the soil of our communities across the continent.

The Audubon movement began almost a century ago. It is the story of ordinary people who took a stand and made a difference. To this day, Audubon's adherents are people who have done what they could, where they were, with the tools available. Conservation's accomplishments of the last hundred years are those of a popular movement, and the triumphs celebrated in this beautiful volume are ones in which we can all share.

Poised on the brink of the millennium, as we anticipate conservation's next century, the challenges we face are not as clear. Urban sprawl, global warming, and overpopulation are daunting problems, seemingly insuperable. To understand how to tackle these uncertainties, we need to learn from an examination of our past achievements.

As you read these remarkable essays, you will come to the realization that although the issues Audubon faced were varied and complex, one element remained constant: the people. Those who effected change did so by acting on a shared vision of a world that still possessed untouched places. People became involved by changing their habits, writing their representatives, demanding safe food and clean water, monitoring bird populations, or acting as watchdogs for the environment.

Our environment's problems will continue to be solved only by the hard work and dedication of individuals like you, who do what they can with what they have, wherever they are. The conservationists of tomorrow may not wield influence singly, but working together, they will make the world understand that humanity cannot flourish without keeping nature intact.

JOHN FLICKER
President, National Audubon Society
March 4, 1999

Introduction: *Speaking for Nature*

by Les Line

THE STORIES ON THE FOLLOWING PAGES are about heroes sung and unsung. About men and women who over the past 100 years devoted and even gave their lives to the cause of conservation in America. Decade by decade, focusing on one or two key issues from each period, the essays chronicle hard-won battles that defined the Audubon movement from its birth during the days of bird slaughter by the plume and market hunters to the ongoing fight to preserve more than token remnants of the country's original forests.

The authors of these ten chapters are longtime contributors to *Audubon* magazine who, beginning in the mid-1960s with the rebirth of the magazine, reported firsthand on such matters.They, too, are heroes, like the conservation leaders, politicians, scientists and—most of all—the indefatigable grassroots activists who are celebrated in these narratives. Indeed, if this book has a flaw, it is the fact that inadequate tribute has been paid to the writers, photographers, and painters who have influenced the way we think about—and behave toward—the natural world. Artists with words, film, and canvas, they truly have been the ones speaking for nature.

The ability to win over hearts and minds to the protection of wild places and wild things is a fairly recent phenomenon. The seeds were planted by two giant figures of the nineteenth century: the artist-ornithologist, John James Audubon and the author-naturalist, Henry David Thoreau. Audubon's 435 watercolors for his *Birds of America* transmitted a sense of the living creatures with an intensity that no one had ever before achieved. His birds, dramatically posed in their natural elements, virtually take flight from the pages of his monumental Double Elephant Folio. So famous is this masterwork that we forget that Audubon also produced a similar portfolio of the continent's mammals, from the lumbering prairie bison to the smallest woodland shrew.

Meanwhile, the writings of Thoreau sustained those who agreed with the philosopher of Walden Pond when he said, "I love Nature partly because she is not a man, but a retreat from him." And exactly 100 years after his death in 1862, eight words by Thoreau—*In wildness is the preservation of the world*—became the rallying cry of the wilderness preservation movement

No surprise, then, that as the nineteenth century ended, the fledgling bird protection movement turned to illustrated publications aimed at adults and children to get its message across. The point is nicely illustrated by examining early issues of *Bird-Lore*—the predecessor of *Audubon*. The journal was founded in 1899 by the distinguished ornithologist, Frank M. Chapman, as an organ for the various state Audubon Societies, and *Bird-Lore* even used poetry at times to lift the ideals of its readers, though Walt Whitman would have grimaced if he had read these lines:

Which would you choose for life's short whirl
The girl with the gun or the camera girl?

The page was illustrated with a drawing of a young lady with a box camera and another with a shotgun, hunting quail. The magazine eventually (and perhaps wisely) gave up publishing poetry until the 1970s, when *Audubon* introduced its audience to the verse of such heralded writers as Ray Bradbury of science fiction fame and the naturalist-essayist, Loren Eiseley.

Nor were *Bird-Lore*'s early efforts in bird photography particularly memorable. In the journal's first two years, it ran eighty-eight pictures of stuffed birds (sometimes in natural-looking dioramas created by Chapman for the American Museum of Natural History), and only seventy-six images of living birds, most of them taken in zoos. But if the photographs published in the early years of *Bird-Lore* were mediocre or suspect, that wasn't the case with the paintings of Louis Agassiz Fuertes, whom many consider to be the greatest of all bird artists. From 1904 to his tragic death in 1927 in a railroad crossing accident, Fuertes's work appeared in nearly every issue of the journal, often as a full-color frontispiece. His drawings—literally thousands of them—interpreted the living bird in ways that the primitive cameras of the day could not. They introduced a generation of Americans to wildlife conservation in many forms, including colorful bird cards (similar to highly collectible baseball cards) that were distributed in boxes of Arm & Hammer baking soda!

Fuertes also worked a major influence on Roger Tory Peterson, who transformed us into a world of watchers and, more importantly, protectors of every form of life on the planet. S. Dillion Ripley, secretary emeritus of the Smithsonian Institution and an elder of the tribe of American ornithologists, once asked, "What if there had been no Roger Tory Peterson? This question brings to mind imponderables such as whether birds would have become the best-known animals in the world." The Peterson Field Guides, which began in 1934 with a thin little book on bird identification, grew to more than thirty volumes under his editorship. Through the magic of these guides, we became more than just watchers of birds, and a powerful constituency was created not only for woodpeckers and warblers but mice and marmots, butterflies and beetles, treefrogs and turtles, shiners and sea anemones, oaks and orchids. And, of course, their vanishing habitats.

Then there were the eloquent wordsmiths whose stories would grace the pages of *Audubon*, especially in later years. Among them were Hal Borland, Archie Carr, Sigurd Olson, Peter Matthiessen, Paul Brooks, George Misch Sutton, Joseph Wood Krutch, Edwin Way Teale, and John K. Terres, a predecessor at the *Audubon* editorship. The force of their words came

Summer residents of the conifer forests of the Pacific Northwest, Townsend's warblers migrate to Mexico and Central America in the winter. (Photo: John Hoffman/Bruce Coleman)

from the fact that they instilled in their readers a love of the world around them, priming them for the environmental crises to come.

Hal Borland, for instance, was born in Nebraska, grew up on the Colorado plains as the son of a small-town newspaper editor, and lived most of his adult life in New England, on a hillside farm along the Housatonic River. He wrote more than thirty books and gained a wide readership—many of it through his Sunday "outdoor editorials" that were an institution in *The New York Times*. Rather than writing of distant places and exotic species, Borland urged people to become acquainted with the common animals and plants around their homes, as suggested by the title of one of his best-known books, *Beyond Your Doorstep*.

The eminent Florida herpetologist, Archie Carr, took his readers farther afield. He roamed the Caribbean, listening to toads and frogs sing their love songs in the night while he searched for elusive answers about the natural history of sea turtles. Some of his most prized essays, one of which won an award as the best short story of the year, are collected in his book, *The Windward Road*.

Sig Olson's beloved landscape was closer to home. He took his canoe into the lakes and rivers of the Far North in the manner of the "voyageurs" of old. So persuasive were such classic books as *The Singing Wilderness* that much of the Quetico-Superior country near Olson's hometown of Ely, Minnesota, is permanently protected.

And when a life-threatening crisis arrived in the form of chemical pesticides, it was another articulate and persuasive voice who altered the course of history with one of the most influential books of our time. A marine scientist with the U.S. Fish and Wildlife

Big Cypress National Reserve in the Florida Everglades is a landscape of sawgrass, palms, and cypress hammocks. (Photo: Jeff Greenberg/Photo Researchers)

Service, Rachel Carson was known for her beautifully written books such as *The Sea Around Us*. She also was a very private person, but with the publication of *Silent Spring* in 1962, this courageous woman subjected herself to incredible abuse from an agricultural-chemical industry whose profits were threatened. She later commented, "Some awareness of this problem has been in the air but the ideas had to be crystallized, the facts had to be brought together in one place. If I had not written the book, I am sure the ideas would have found another outlet. But knowing the facts as I did, I could not rest until I had brought them to public attention."

Finally, there are the artists whose canvas today is usually—though not always—color film. The first great wild bird photographer was William L. Finley from Oregon who, among his other achievements, photographed California condors in 1906 with a cumbersome glass plate camera that he lugged into their remote and rugged nesting place. The fragile plates alone were a back-breaking load: the equivalent of a roll of today's 35mm Kodachrome would weigh twelve pounds. Yet it wasn't unusual to find Finley in the top of a towering Douglas fir, photographing a western tanager's nest, or far out on a sycamore limb at a golden eagle aerie.

In the late 1950s, an outwardly gruff former businessman from New Jersey, Frederick Kent Truslow, led bird photography into the new 35mm era. Pushed into early retirement by his doctor, Truslow unilaterally decided that he would become a *National Geographic* photographer and he refused to be politely shuffled out the door by the editors. Truslow had a winter home near Everglades National Park and soon the magazine's pages featured his marvelous images of species like the strange snail-eating limpkin, whose piercing wail rends the sawgrass world at night. Fred Truslow's monumental achievement was documenting the long nesting season of the then-disappearing bald eagle. Every morning before daybreak, for weeks on end, he entered a canvas blind atop a hand-erected tower on a Florida Bay mangrove island. Enduring wilting heat, insect hordes, and deadly snakes, Truslow returned with images of our national bird that have never been surpassed.

The film, camera, and telephoto lenses that Truslow used forty years ago are prehistoric compared to the high-tech equipment carried by his successors whose work is represented in these pages, and some of the pictures we see in magazines today are nothing short of extraordinary. (However, Truslow would have exploded at the idea of using tame rental animals and staged settings, a practice common among competitive wildlife photographers today, or manipulating images with computers, as some do.) Meanwhile, it was time for a small group of artists who were documenting the American wilderness with large-format view cameras—not all that different from William Finley's—to play a decisive role in the modern conservation story.

It was the celebrated landscape photographer, Ansel Adams, who urged David Brower, the Sierra Club's executive director, to create an Exhibit Format series of books that would focus on America's threatened wild places. The series began in 1962 with a now-classic volume matching the masterful compositions of Eliot Porter with appropriate quotations from the writings of Thoreau. The title, of course, was *In Wildness Is the Preservation of the World*. Brower spared no expense in producing these lavish picture books, and eventually the Sierra Club's publishing program ran into financial difficulty. But the important role the books played in such landmark battles as blocking dams in the Grand Canyon, creating a Redwoods National Park and another in the North Cascades, and establishing the first wilderness areas cannot be measured on a spreadsheet.

These spectacular books also helped inspire the re-creation of *Audubon* as a magazine that would introduce its readers to writing about natural history as literature, not simply information; to nature photography and painting as art, not just illustration. A magazine that would cover environmental stories as journalists should, without the baggage of institutional beliefs or propaganda. And a magazine that would nourish an army of writers, artists, and photographers to provide those eloquent and incisive words, those memorable images, and who would speak for nature and lead others to the cause.

A final note about words. *Conservation* is a venerable term that is often defined as the "wise use of natural resources," a phrase that surely embraces air and water as firmly as the various pieces of the landscape mosaic, like forests and prairies and the lifeforms they support. But after the first Earth Day in 1970, with its focus on the abuse of the human environment, we became known as *environmentalists*, and in the corners of the conservation community there was a not-so-subtle shift of emphasis away from the traditional role of protecting wildlife and wild places. By 1990, a private-sector ecocrat in Washington, D.C., confidently told the press: "The old school of conservationists who were interested in wildlife for wildlife's sake is dying out. We're left with a populace that is interested in the environment to a degree that it touches their private lives, i.e. waste disposal."

I would challenge that statement, if only for the fact that conservation, or if you prefer, environmentalism, demands the kind of passion that comes from a love and concern for eagles and prairie dogs, turtles and salmon, orchids and towering Douglas firs, not landfills and recycling. To paraphrase Thoreau, in *wonder* is the preservation of the world. And we will always need artists with word, film, and canvas to lead us.

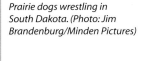

***Opposite:** The Brahma and Zoroaster Temples are framed by autumn foliage on the north rim of the Grand Canyon. (Photo: Tom Bean)*

Prairie dogs wrestling in South Dakota. (Photo: Jim Brandenburg/Minden Pictures)

1900

The Age of Extermination

1900

The Age of Extermination

by Frank Graham Jr.

IN THE SPRING OF 1885 three youthful adventurers penetrated the sawgrass wilderness of Florida's Everglades by sloop and canoe. The sloop's owner, twenty-one-year-old Charles William Pierce of Miami, kept a log of the expedition that provided the human element for the opening act in the drama that was to become the wildlife conservation movement in America.

"After a late getup this morning, and a later breakfast, we went back to the rookery for more plumes," Pierce wrote one evening. "Guy was feeling so much better he also took a hand in the shooting. I was sitting in the bushes waiting for the birds to come, when one settled in the bush not ten feet above me, it stretched its neck to get a better look at me, I shot at the neck and cut it clean off, the head fell in the mud at my feet. Louie killed eleven birds, Guy killed eight, and I killed nineteen. It took us all the rest of the day to prepare the skins and dry them. We would like to stay here until we have killed all the birds, but I have promised to be [home] at the end of five days."

Pierce, in his log, set the scene for the drama. He also sketched in the protagonists—the herons and egrets with their long legs and their gorgeous white plumes, and the three youths who stand in here for the thousands of gunners all over the country who massacred these "plume birds" for the millinery industry. In a final stroke, Pierce introduced, in the person of one of his chums, the sixteen-year-old Guy Bradley who was to lose his life twenty years later in an attempt to protect the few remaining plume birds in the Everglades.

The nineteenth century was "The Age of Extermination" in North America. For most Europeans in the New World, animals were for shooting. They killed wolves and grizzly bears out of fear, ducks and deer for food, beavers and seals for fur, alligators for leather, and buffalo often for fun—or worse, to deprive the Plains Indians of their sustenance. Venturing onto the oceans, the newcomers pursued the great whales for oil and whalebone. Toward the century's close the killing was also driven by what seems now a trivial compulsion: to ornament hats and dresses with the feathers of wild birds.

A feather is an astonishing blend of utility and beauty. Its myriad barbs and barbules (tiny hooked appendages) bind a bird's plumage into a compact wall against rain and cold, while its form and coloring—whether of subtle shadings or outrageous splashes of yellow and vermillion—fascinate the human eye.

And then there is an age-old idea that whatever is glorious to behold must be possessed. Warriors from the beginning of time used feathers to adorn their headgear, and artists have endlessly reproduced in paintings the shining helmets of European military officers topped with sprays of plumes, and the long, prestigious headdresses of native

Pages 20-21: The black-crowned night heron is heard more often than seen. Unlike most other North American herons, this stocky, short-necked species forages after dusk falls on the marsh, making its presence known with a harsh barking call. By sunrise these herons are roosting in reeds or trees, like this bird in Shark Valley in Everglades National Park. (Photo: Arthur Morris/Birds As Art)

Page 23: Nearly all of the world's sixty heron species use the time-proven, stand-and-wait technique when fishing. With remarkable patience, they let their prey swim within reach of a lightning-fast bill strike. One exception is the reddish egret, whose stronghold is the Texas coastal islands. These handsome herons dash about the shallows while flicking their wings to startle hidden prey into leaving their cover. A shaggy, rufous head and neck explain the name, but the reddish egret also has a rare white color phase. (Photo: Arthur Morris/Birds As Art)

Opposite: A great egret displays before its mate, fanning the nuptial plumes that, like the bright green facial skin, appear only during the breeding season. A century ago, these filamentous aigrettes were coveted by the millinery trade and few heron rookeries escaped a bloodbath at the hands of plume hunters. Public outrage over the slaughter led to the formation of the first Audubon Societies. (Photo: Arthur Morris/Birds As Art)

Top, left: Everglades National Park appears utterly wild and pristine from the air. But immediately after the park was created in 1947, the U.S. Army Corps of Engineers began diverting the freshwater flow for the benefit of agriculture and development interests, upsetting the 'Glades ecology. Now, the Corps has an $8 billion plan to remove the dikes and plug drainage canals in order to restore some of that historic sheet-flow by the year 2022. (Photo: Daniel J. Cox/Natural Exposures)

Top, right: Milliners tried to dupe the public into believing that their outlandish creations were made with feathers plucked from living birds, but by one estimate, 200 million birds were killed world-wide in one year to supply the fashion trade. (Photo: Library of Congress)

Americans. The Roman elite are said to have prized flyswatters made from peacocks' tails. Queen Marie Antoinette (called "Featherhead" by her brother Joseph) touched off a fashionable craze at the pre-revolution French court by inserting the feathers of peacocks and ostriches into her hairdo; soon those towering feathery displays forced fashionable women to ride with their heads sticking out the windows of their low-roofed carriages.

The millinery industry, through contemporary fashion magazines, rekindled the craze as the nineteenth century progressed. The feathers most in demand were those of the herons and egrets. Especially prized were the aigrettes, or long plumes, that grow only in the breeding season, from between the shoulders and extending to or beyond the tail of the snowy egret. These silky, tapered feathers, with shafts six or seven inches long, are recurved at the tip and tend to wave gracefully in the lightest breeze. By the last two decades of the century, popular magazines such as *Godey's Lady's Book* featured illustrations of outlandish millinery displays, with hats bearing showy "confections" of lace, ribbons, plumes, and even a stuffed, glassy-eyed bird.

Although the milliners often contended that the plumes were simply "plucked" from live birds, the truth was far less humane. Gunners killed millions of wild birds all over the world to supply the fashion markets. As Charles Pierce and his young friends learned in the Everglades, the millinery gunners would scalp the birds after shooting them, then make a slit "about halfway up the neck, and skin down to the tail, taking all the skin off the body, and out to the first joint of the wing, then rub the skins with cornmeal and stretch them with small sticks until dry." At that point they shipped the skins, with their plumes intact, to the milliners.

Through the late 1880s, one enterprising collector of birds in Florida had sixty hunters working for him and was taking perhaps 150 birds a day. A waterfowl hunter on New York's Long Island sold gulls' wings to Macy's Department Store for eleven cents a pair and shipped the rest of his feathers to manufacturers of fishing supplies, who turned them into flies for anglers. A millinery dealer in New York,

having received an order from Paris for 40 thousand birdskins, hired hunters on the Virginia coast to kill terns at ten cents apiece. Other milliners paid fishermen and American Indians to shoot gulls and terns at their colonies on Maine's islands. Later researchers put the number of birds killed worldwide for the millinery trade in 1900 at 200 million.

Yet even that figure does not cover the extent of the carnage. Hunters went after many species, including the herons and egrets, only during the breeding season when the birds gathered in closely clustered colonies and their nuptial plumes were at their most resplendent. After killing the adults, the hunters left the chicks to starve and rot in the sun. Joining the millinery gunners in the slaughter were thousands of hunters who supplied wild birds for restaurants, hotels, and food markets. Observers tell of visiting markets where even small species such as robins and bobolinks hung from strings in clusters "like onions."

"This daily exhibition in southern markets," wrote the ornithologist J. A. Allen, "indicates an immense destruction of northern breeding song birds which resort to the southern states for a winter home."

Reaction to the slaughter was slow to come.

These Forster's terns were paired before they arrived at their breeding place on New Jersey's Cape May. But courtship continues through nest building, egg-laying, and incubation, with the male regularly bringing minnows to his demanding mate in order to prove his loyalty. Tern colonies along the Atlantic Coast were also raided by plume hunters and it wasn't uncommon in the early 1900s to see a fashionable woman wearing a hat decorated with an entire skin from the orange bill to the deeply forked tail. (Photo: Arthur Morris/Birds As Art)

Alexander Wilson, the "Father of American Ornithology," was one of the first to express dismay at the dwindling populations of birds of all kinds. Early in the nineteenth century he told of a "humane person" (thought by historians to be Wilson himself) who stopped the killing of robins for food around Boston by writing an anonymous paragraph for a newspaper, suggesting that those birds fed on poisonous berries.

Even John James Audubon, the great painter of birds, boasted of his prowess as a sportsman, and his writings sometimes reverberate with the crack of rifles rather than the songs of birds. Of one excursion to hunt herons and other wading birds on the incoming tide in Florida, he wrote: "Each of us, provided with a gun, posted himself behind a blind, and no sooner had the water forced the winged creatures to approach the shore than the work of destruction commenced. When it at length ceased, the collected mass of birds of different kinds looked not unlike a small haycock."

But Audubon eventually began to feel pangs of regret as the great flocks of birds he knew as a young man disappeared from the landscape. Finally, in 1886, George Bird Grinnell, the editor of the sportsman's magazine, *Forest and Stream,* worried in print about the destruction and formed a society named for the painter to campaign for a nationwide change of heart. But this Audubon Society, as well as the magazine he created a year later, quickly expired and he gave up his crusade in discouragement.

A reservoir of sympathy remained, however, ready to be tapped by some as yet unknown organizational force. The occasional laws passed by state legislatures to protect birds were rare and mostly ineffectual. For a time the best hope seemed to lie with the full-time ornithologists, who had formed their own organization in 1883. The American Ornithologists' Union (AOU), in fact, drew up a so-called model law on which it urged the various states to base protective legislation of their own.

Ironically, the ornithologists were much too divided on the issue to put their own law into effect.

***Right:** The pioneer ornithologist, Alexander Wilson (1766-1813), roamed the wilds of eastern North America on horseback, on foot, and by boat well ahead of John James Audubon, painting 262 species for his* American Ornithology. *Wilson's life's work would be overshadowed by Audubon's, but more bird species still bear his name, including Wilson's phalarope and Wilson's warbler. (Photo courtesy of the Massachusetts Audubon Society)*

***Far right:** Like Wilson, John James Audubon (1785-1851) was portrayed with gun in hand, and some revisionists would depict him as a butcher rather than a painter of birds. It's true that he shot a great many birds—for food, for sport, for science. But while binoculars and cameras with autofocus telephoto lenses are tools of present-day bird artists, the only way Audubon could get a closer look was with his trusty shotgun. (Photo: Corbis-Bettmann)*

Many members were not professional scientists in the modern sense but, rather, commercial taxidermists or amateur egg collectors who believed such laws to be aimed at themselves. Even some scientists were hostile. "I don't protect birds," one ornithologist remarked, "I kill them."

It was true that in the fever to collect new or rare birds, the museum specialists sometimes contributed to the eclipse of a species. Consider the Bachman's warbler. Audubon himself had first collected this very rare little bird in 1833 and named it for John Bachman, a South Carolina minister and naturalist. The species was not recorded again until 1886, when a plume-hunter shot seven of them in Louisiana. Then, in 1890, two of the country's most eminent ornithologists, William Brewster and Frank M. Chapman, collected forty-six Bachman's warblers along Florida's Suwannee River. Another ornithologist bagged fifty more there the following year. A modern ornithologist has commented drily: "The species has never been reported in such numbers anywhere again, and it has not been seen in Florida since 1909." The species is probably extinct.

The true beginnings of the wildlife protection movement in the United States can be traced to a precise place and time. Harriet Hemenway was a member of a prominent Massachusetts family and shared a lively interest in the outdoors with her husband Augustus, likewise a wealthy and civic-minded Bostonian for whom the Hemenway Gymnasium at Harvard was named. After reading an article about the killing of birds for the plume trade in Florida, Harriet Hemenway decided that something ought to be done about it. She and her cousin, Minna B. Hall, began to go through a copy of *The Boston Blue Book.*

"We marked the ladies of fashion who would be likely to wear aigrettes on their hats or in their hair," Hall afterward recalled. "We then sent out circulars asking the women to join a society for the protection of birds, especially the egret. Some women joined and some who preferred to wear the feathers would not."

On February 10, 1896, the meeting took place at the Hemenway home at 273 Clarendon Street in Boston. Among those present, besides notables from the *Blue Book,* were several prominent ornithologists. The participants formed a society that they hoped would spread the good word about saving wild birds and influence the state legislature. In making plans, they reached for the name that George Bird Grinnell had made almost synonymous with bird protection and called their organization the Massachusetts Audubon Society.

This time the idea caught on. Reformers, naturalists, civic leaders, and school teachers added their names to the growing list of Audubon members. Other states formed their own Audubon Societies. The Audubon Society of the District of Columbia named as its first president George Miller Sternberg, Surgeon General of the United States Army, while Assistant Secretary of the Navy Theodore Roosevelt accepted an honorary membership.

Page 28: *A dapper little bird of swampy lowland forests, Bachman's warbler was discovered and painted by Audubon, who named the species for his friend, John Bachman, a South Carolina minister and fellow naturalist. Bachman's warbler may be extinct, in part because of heavy collecting by ornithologists in the late nineteenth century. No nest has been found since 1937 despite intensive searches, although there are occasional reports of sightings. (Photo courtesy of the National Audubon Society)*

Pages 28-29: *A tricolored heron lurks among the stiltlike roots of saltwater-tolerant red mangroves at Ding Darling National Wildlife Refuge in Florida. Because this slender, graceful bird was largely ignored by hunters, who preferred to gather the egrets' snowy plumes, it may be the most common heron from Florida to Texas. Tricolored herons breed in large colonies of a thousand or more pairs, building their stick nests on or close to the ground. (Photo: John Shaw)*

Opposite: *An elaborate ceremony in which a male great blue heron offers a carefully chosen leafy twig to his mate, for addition to the nest, helps maintain the pair bond, even after incubation has begun. During the courtship period, the male builds (or rebuilds) a rough platform to help attract a mate, but she will complete the nest. Displays like this are repeated a dozen or more times a day early in the nesting season but become perfunctory after the chicks hatch. (Photo: Arthur Morris/Birds As Art)*

"The conservation of our natural resources and their proper use constitute the fundamental problem which underlies almost every other problem of our national life," Theodore Roosevelt declared to Congress in 1907. As president for the first eight years of this century, Roosevelt did not just talk about conservation from his bully pulpit. He threw the full weight of his office behind conservation, and he put the issue at the top of the country's agenda.

Beginning with Pelican Island in eastern Florida, Roosevelt created the national wildlife refuge system, which included fifty-one biologically significant sites by the time he left office. He expanded the national forests from 42 million acres to 172 million and preserved eighteen acres as national monuments, including the Grand Canyon and the Petrified Forest. It gave him immense satisfaction to know that "these bits of the old wilderness scenery and the old wilderness life were to be kept unspoiled for the benefit of our children's children." Roosevelt was an avid camper and hiker. Yet he conserved not for nature's sake, though he thought that a worthwhile goal, but for people's. He reminded everyone who would listen that restricting grazing and logging on steep slopes protected watersheds, which provided drinking and irrigation water and flood control. The national forests, to his mind, preserved trees less for their beauty than to ensure a stable supply of lumber for home building.

As Senator Robert La Follette of Wisconsin said of Roosevelt in the twilight of his presidency, "His greatest work was actually beginning a world movement for staying terrestrial waste and saving for the human race the things upon which alone a great and peaceful and progressive and happy race can be founded."

—David Seideman

Bird protection suddenly became popular. Frank M. Chapman of the American Museum of Natural History traveled to Washington to lecture local society on the topic "Woman as a Bird Enemy." The Pennsylvania Audubon Society published a pamphlet entitled "Woman's Heartlessness," which had been written by the poet Celia Thaxter before her death in 1894. Thaxter recounted her argument with a cultivated but uncaring woman who insisted on wearing plumes. "It was merely a waste of breath," the poet concluded, "and she went her way, a charnel house of beaks and claws and bones and feathers and glass eyes upon her fatuous head."

By the turn of the century the bird protection movement had acquired a strong leader. William Dutcher—a successful businessman in New York City who was both a hunter and a reputable amateur ornithologist, the treasurer of the AOU, and the most enterprising member of its bird protection committee—was eminently qualified for the role. Rather than focus his attack on "heartless women" or backwoods plume hunters, Dutcher singled out the millinery industry, which was centered in New York. He believed that only national legislation that eliminated the plumage of wild birds from commerce could effectively preserve American birdlife.

Congress, in fact, took the first step in that direction in 1900 when it passed, with the active support of Dutcher and the rest of the bird protectors, the Lacey Act. This legislation invoked the "commerce clause" of the United States Constitution (which gives the federal government the authority to regulate interstate commerce in goods) to prohibit the shipment from one state to another of birds and other animals killed in violation of state laws.

Dutcher considered this act a handy tool, but not sufficient at the moment for his purposes. Most states did not yet have effective laws against the killing of birds. He then turned to other tools in an attempt to slow down the killing until the various states enacted the model law. He believed in both education and restraint, writing dozens of pamphlets to make use of the spreading concern for birds and seeking the means of guarding important bird colonies. In those campaigns Dutcher found valuable allies in Frank M. Chapman at the American Museum and Abbott Thayer, a well-known New England painter and naturalist.

Chapman had founded the publication *Bird-Lore* (which was to evolve decades later into the most celebrated of all nature magazines, *Audubon*). From the beginning he devoted space in *Bird-Lore* to news from the various state Audubon societies that numbered thirty-five by the turn of the century. As another educational device, Chapman introduced in 1900 the first Christmas Bird Count to replace the traditional holiday hunting sprees, when revelers set out to shoot birds. Chapman's use of interesting natural history articles and photographs sweetened the conservation message that Dutcher fed him. (A later naturalist pointed out that of the 164 bird photographs appearing during the magazine's first two years of publication, 88 were of stuffed specimens and, of the rest, many had been taken in zoos.)

In the same year, Abbott Thayer contacted colleagues in the AOU and offered to raise money for wardens who would protect the most-endangered

The noted New England painter and naturalist, Abbott Thayer, raised money in 1900 for wardens to protect nesting colonies of terns and gulls along the Maine coast. (Photo: Corbis/Bettmann)

nesting colonies. Some members were skeptical, but Dutcher accepted Thayer's idea. He decided to focus on Maine, where milliners were supplying Indians with guns and ammunition to kill gulls and their smaller relatives, the terns, on offshore islands.

"There is no law protecting the gulls along our Maine coast, and they may be shot anywhere, even in the harbor of Bangor where they come fall and spring," Dutcher wrote to Thayer. "The fishermen shoot hundreds of all the gulls that occur by using a sneak boat which is disguised to resemble a lot of drift stuff, and by gradually skulling this up to a flock of gulls can secure a number 'ere they take aloft."

Dutcher traveled widely in Maine in the early 1900s, lobbying for passage of the model law and lining up lighthouse keepers to serve as wardens at their stations and on nearby islands. That the job was not without risk became apparent when the lightkeeper on Great Duck Island off Bar Harbor, who had posted the island against trespassers, was openly defied by millinery gunners landing there. "But their work is in the night," the lightkeeper wrote Dutcher. "I cannot learn their names. If I had a Kodak I could

The lighthouse on Cape Neddick is typical of the stations along the wild and rocky Maine shore whose keepers were among the first Audubon wardens. (Photo: John Shaw)

get their faces or catch them in the act. But I had rather shoot them. Posters don't count."

By 1901 Maine and ten other states had passed new bird protection laws or strengthened existing ones. Thayer funneled money to Dutcher and extended the warden system to Virginia. The program was working, as gulls and terns returned to protected islands and produced chicks for the first time in years. But the Deep South remained a plume-hunter's paradise. The presence of a small but enthusiastic Florida Audubon Society and a version of the model law had made little impact on the hunters because protection was inadequate in the field. Most of the heronries, including the remote Cuthbert Rookery in the Everglades, had been shot out.

An active Audubon member urged the prompt hiring of a warden. "The game warden to deal with this situation must be a resident," he wrote, "well acquainted with local conditions, a strong, fearless man and one fully alive to the value of bird protection. Fortunately for the birds and for us, I found residing at Cape Sable [at Florida's southern tip] a man who combines in himself all these requirements. He is Mr. Guy Bradley, a young, recently married man, brought up from earliest childhood on the east coast of Florida, a thorough woodsman, a plume hunter by occupation before the passage of the present law, since which time, as I have ample testimony, he has not killed a bird. . . . I have known these Bradley boys for many years and can honestly say that I know of no better man for game warden in the whole state of Florida than Guy."

Bradley was the same "Guy" who had accompanied the young Charles Pierce into the 'Glades to shoot plume birds many years before. The word about his skills was duly passed on to William Dutcher in New York and, acting on the ancient wisdom that the best keeper of the henhouse is a reformed fox, he hired Bradley as an AOU warden at $36 dollars a month. That Bradley was no bumpkin is demonstrated by the careful nature of the reports he sent to Dutcher in the next couple of years.

Meanwhile, Dutcher had grown impatient at the lack of progress in passing legislation on the state and national levels. The AOU, divided on the issue of a strong model law, was unable to mobilize public

***Pages 34-35:** By 1918, when Congress passed a landmark law prohibiting the market hunting of migratory birds, the plume frenzy had mostly dissipated. But the slaughter of birds for fashion had its counterpart a half-century later when hide-hunters decimated American alligator populations across the Southeast to provide leather for luxurious handbags, belts, and shoes. The poachers were put out of business by the Endangered Species Act of 1973 and a clampdown on illegal traffic in alligator skins. Like the herons and egrets, populations of the big armored reptiles have recovered significantly under federal and state protection. (Photo: Daniel J. Cox/Natural Exposures)*

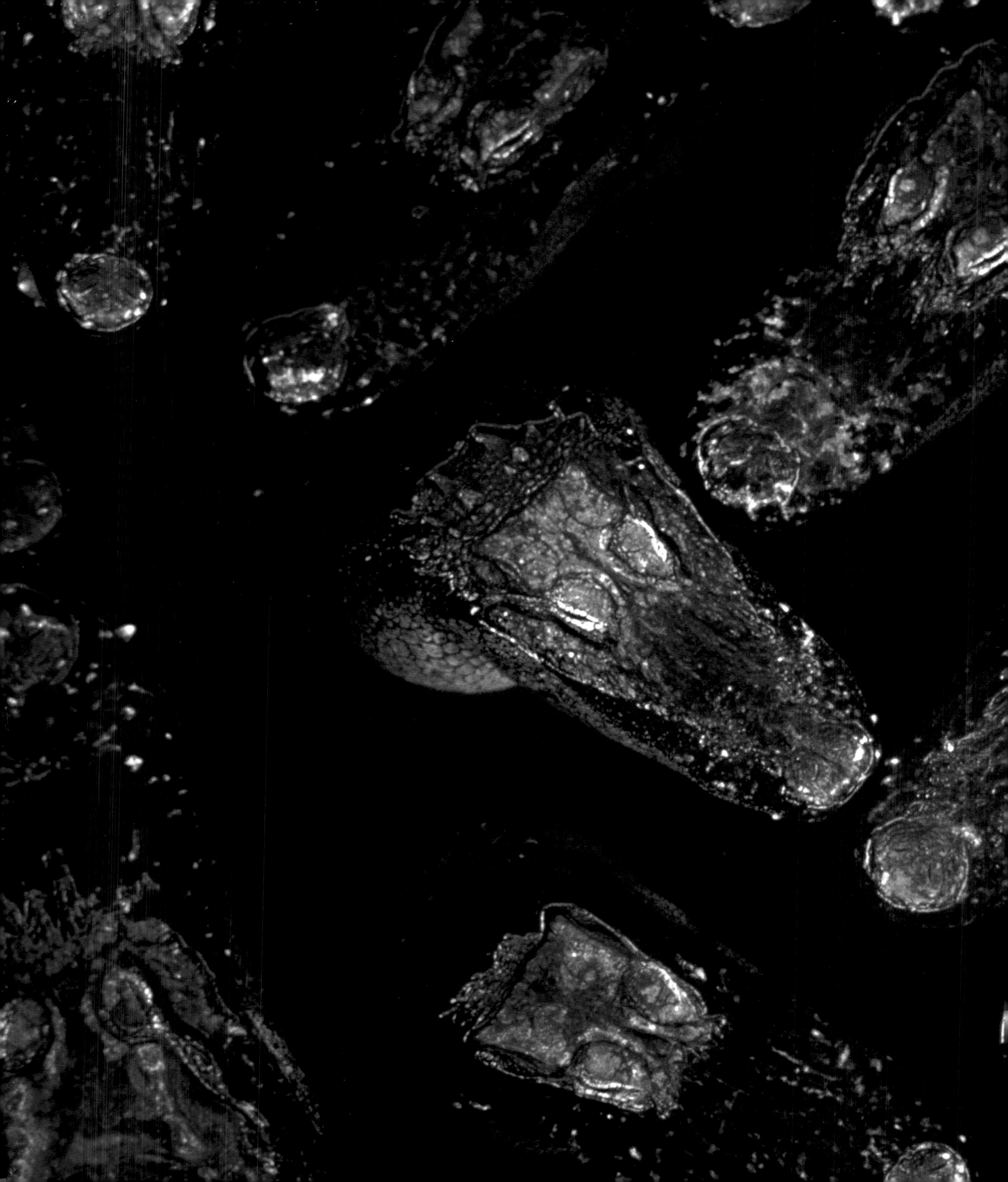

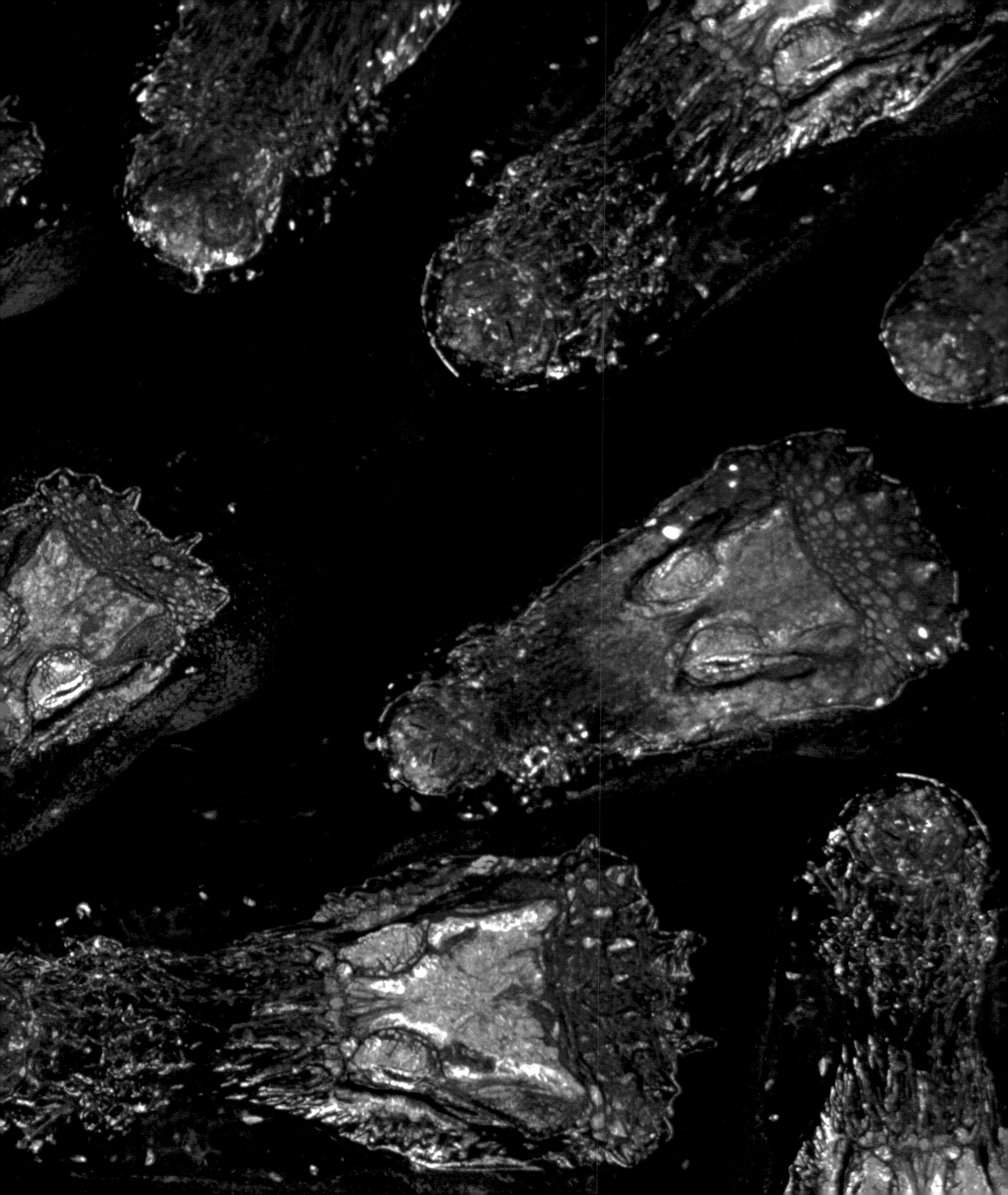

Opposite, top: *Two great egrets scrap over a choice territory at a Florida rookery which might support the nests of as many as seven different heron species. To avoid interspecies competition for sites, great blue herons nest high in the trees, great egrets settle into the understory, and late-arriving snowy egrets and tricolored herons build their platforms fairly close to the water or ground. (Photo: Carl R. Sams II)*

Opposite, bottom: *The roseate spoonbill is a tactile forager. That is, its unusual banjo-shaped bill, which the bird sweeps through knee-deep water in wide arcs, snaps shut as a reflex action when contact with prey stimulates nerves at the tip. This spoonbill on the Texas coast is in full breeding regalia, notably the splashes of crimson feathers that account for the folk name, flame bird. (Photo: Tim Fitzharris/Minden Pictures)*

opinion. But the presence of thirty-five state Audubon societies suggested to Dutcher that his best chance for a united front lay with the amateurs. It certainly helped that, for the first time in the nation's history, an enthusiastic birdwatcher occupied the White House. President Theodore Roosevelt had been closely involved with natural history projects since he was a boy, and now kept a list of birds he spotted on the White House grounds. In 1903, at the urging of Dutcher and Chapman, Roosevelt set aside the first federal bird refuge on Florida's Pelican Island.

The time was ripe. Having organized the state societies in a loose committee, Dutcher then moved to build a strong federation. Representatives of the various societies met in New York (an appropriate locale since the city's millinery industry was Dutcher's chief target) and on January 5, 1905, approved the incorporation of the National Association of Audubon Societies for the Protection of Wild Birds and Animals. Dutcher was elected its president.

One of the new organization's most important steps was the hiring of T. Gilbert Pearson, an energetic educator and lobbyist from North Carolina who became Dutcher's assistant and later his successor. He was the quintessential "good ol' boy," one who knew his way around legislatures and could wheel and deal with the best of them. For the rest of the decade Pearson pressed for sound laws and enforcement in New York as well as in the Deep South, which remained the last refuge of both the plume birds and

The rollicking yucca-yucca-yucca cry of the herring gull can be heard over the pounding of waves on the Maine coast. Although this elegant seabird's breeding colonies were once plundered by plume hunters, the herring gull population in New England has exploded because of the easy availability of food at garbage dumps. The gulls are mainly scavengers, but they also eat the eggs and young of other birds, and biologists use various control tactics to protect the nests of terns from their formidable neighbors. (Photo Les Line)

their hunters. Enforcement was still a major obstacle to protection in the South's rural areas. The warden system devised by Dutcher and Thayer had paid dividends at vulnerable island colonies of gulls and terns along the northern and middle Atlantic coasts, and now Pearson began to extend it through the southern states.

With the incorporation of the state societies, Guy Bradley became an Audubon warden, taking time off from his work as a land surveyor. He was in his mid-thirties, strong and deeply tanned, the father of two children. Regularly he patrolled the waters off southern Florida in a naphtha-powered motor launch, provided by the state society and named the *Audubon*. Then, on July 8, 1905, when the new association was barely six months old, Bradley observed several men land on Oyster Key, a small island in Florida Bay that was home to a flock of egrets. He must have recognized among the men a plume hunter he had arrested earlier.

The warden rowed out to the men's schooner just as they returned with dead birds. When he tried to arrest them, one of the men fired a shot at Bradley, killing him instantly. His body fell back into his boat. Later, some residents of Cape Sable noticed turkey vultures circling over the drifting boat and discovered the body.

Although no one was ever found guilty of the murder, relatives of Bradley's widow burned the house of the chief suspect and word of the tragedy spread across the country to touch the public's consciousness, perhaps even its conscience. Women's clubs voted to discourage the use of plumes and urged others to do the same. A national magazine carried a feature article entitled "Bird Protection's First Martyr." And in New York Dutcher received a message from President Roosevelt: "Permit me on behalf of both Mrs. Roosevelt and myself to say how heartily we sympathize not only with the work of the Audubon Societies generally, but particularly in their efforts to stop the sale and use of the so-called aigrettes—the plumes of the white herons. If anything, Mrs. Roosevelt feels more strongly than I do in the matter."

As the century's first decade came to an end, the young bird-protection movement made major breakthroughs in state legislatures, which soon brought about a ban on the sale of the flesh and feathers of wild birds. These triumphs led inevitably to the Migratory Bird Treaty Act of 1918, ratifying an agreement with Canada that prohibited the killing of most kinds of North American birds and approved regulations governing the sport hunting of game species.

A remarkable change had come over the nation's outlook toward its wild heritage since that day, decades earlier, when Charles Pierce led the Bradley boys into the Everglades on their grim mission. In his log, Pierce recalled an evening when the three of them were finishing supper and two white ibises flew over their remote camp, their long necks and arched bills pointed like graceful prows toward the setting sun.

"They were out of reach of our guns," he wrote, "so all we could do was to admire their beauty and watch them go." A great range of feeling was already present, waiting for a powerful new movement that would come forward and nurture it.

Opposite: *Golden slippers are the trademark of the snowy egret, a dainty heron a bit more than half the size of the great egret, emblem of the National Audubon Society. The snowy egret was nearly shot into extinction for its breeding finery but has since expanded its range well north of its former limits, even nesting in Maine. An active rather than a patient hunter, the snowy will sprint about a pond, pausing frequently to stir up prey with its feet or lure fish within bill range by flashing its bright yellow toes. (Photo: John Shaw)*

Left: *The green-backed heron is a solitary and secretive bird, about the size of a crow, that haunts the dense woody edges of both freshwater and saltwater ponds, lakes, rivers, and bays. Green-backed herons are typically seen poised on a low branch, leaning forward until the bill nearly touches the water, and sometimes a bird will stab at a fish, miss, lose its balance, topple into the water, and swim right after its prey. (Photo: John Shaw)*

1910

A Common Possession

1910

A Common Possession

by Peter Steinhart

AT THE OUTSET, North America's source of sustenance and wealth was its wild creatures. Some evidence suggests that even before Columbus, British fishermen crossed the Atlantic to exploit American fisheries. In the early settlement of Virginia, Captain John Smith often found farming less reliable than fishing, and boasted of taking fish "with a casting net, thousands when we pleased." He dried the fish and sent them by the boatload for sale in Europe. By 1632 at least 300 ships a year carried dried fish from America to Spain and Portugal.

Before farmers moved west, fur-trappers wrung the beavers from the streams and sent them to European markets. As settlers cleared the forests, they survived on deer and rabbits. As cities grew and hotels and restaurants proliferated, market hunters and commercial fishermen provided quail, duck, venison, and herring for their tables. In 1903 alone, estimated William Finley, Audubon's field representative in Oregon, 120 tons of ducks and geese were shipped from Lower Klamath Lake to markets in San Francisco.

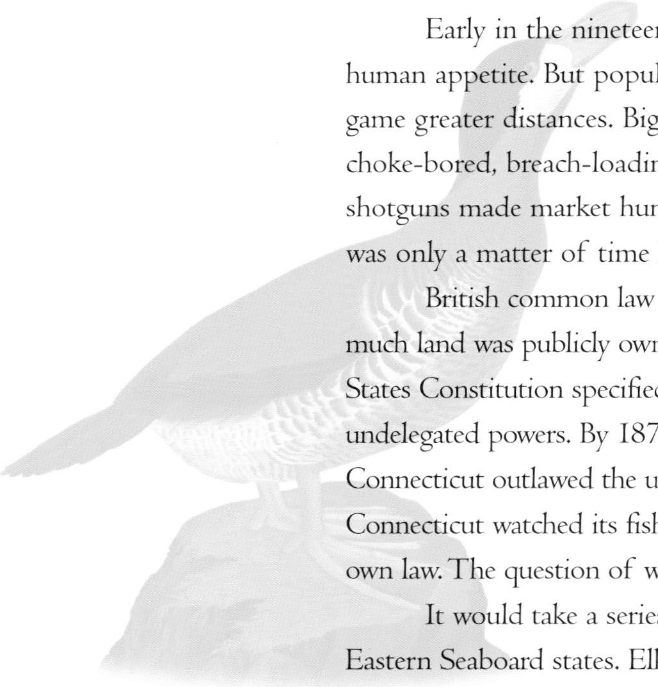

Early in the nineteenth century, population overtook the capacity of fish and wildlife to sustain both itself and human appetite. But population continued to grow, and railroads and refrigeration made it possible to ship fish and game greater distances. Bigger nets and steam engines to winch them in took an even greater toll on fish. In the 1870s, choke-bored, breach-loading shotguns increased the range at which one could effectively hunt, and soon after repeating shotguns made market hunting even more devastating. Clearly, the traditional exploitation could not go on forever. It was only a matter of time before people began to question who owned fish and wildlife: everybody or nobody?

British common law awarded wildlife to whoever owned the land it happened to be visiting; in America, where so much land was publicly owned, that more or less meant it belonged to whoever waylaid it with hook or bullet. The United States Constitution specified no federal authority over fish and wildlife, and the Tenth Amendment reserved to the states all undelegated powers. By 1870, no state had yet asserted that authority. When New England fisheries collapsed in that year, Connecticut outlawed the use of fish traps, but after Massachusetts and Rhode Island failed to enact comparable bans, Connecticut watched its fishermen go hungry while those of neighboring states still put out to sea, and then repealed its own law. The question of who owned wildlife would not be answered until the second decade of the twentieth century.

It would take a series of crises to frame the issue. By the 1870s it was becoming clear that deer were vanishing from Eastern Seaboard states. Elk and antelope were being slaughtered in the West and bison were shot on the Plains with

***Pages 40-41:** Tens of thousands of snow geese, down from their High Arctic breeding grounds, spend the winter months at Bosque del Apache, a national wildlife refuge created in 1939 in the Rio Grande valley near Socorro, New Mexico. The concentrations of geese and other water birds and their spectacular flights at dawn and dusk make the Bosque a must stop for bird-watchers and nature photographers. The dark bird in the top right corner represents a morph or color phase of the snow goose. The "blue goose" was once considered a separate species and is more commonly seen on wintering grounds along the Gulf Coast. (Photo: Arthur Morris/Birds As Art)*

***Page 43:** A bird of western wetlands, the American avocet feeds by sweeping its long, upward-curved bill along the surface of the water, picking up aquatic insects, crustaceans, and other small invertebrates. Avocets are gregarious shorebirds and will mob any hapless predator that comes near a nesting colony. (Photo: Art Wolfe)*

***Opposite, top:** A beaver lunches on the bark of a newly felled poplar tree. By some estimates, there were as many as 400 million beaver in North America before fur-trappers cleaned out the eastern lakes and streams and moved westward in the late 1700s. Trapping regulations and transplant programs have brought beaver back to many of their former haunts. But now these irrepressible dam-builders come into frequent conflict with country homeowners whose property is flooded or whose ornamental trees are gnawed down. (Photo: Daniel J. Cox/Natural Exposures)*

***Opposite, bottom:** Where 50 million American bison once thundered over the Great Plains, by 1900 only a few hundred had survived the long-range rifles of the hide and meat hunters. There are a number of bison herds today on public preserves and private ranches, and this is counted as a major conservation triumph. But essentially the animals live in cages, however large their range might be. For example, wild bison in Yellowstone are shot if they leave national park land because ranchers fear they will spread disease to cattle. (Photo: Jim Brandenburg/Minden Pictures)*

Thanks to William Hornaday, America still has bison. Alarmed because bison herds were dwindling, Hornaday helped acquire breeding stock for a program that contributed to the animal's recovery. Hornaday persuaded President Theodore Roosevelt and Congress to set aside several reserves, among them the 18,500-acre National Bison Range in Montana. He was also influential in halting the hunting of fur seals and sea otters and was founder and then a director of the New York Zoological Society.

William Hornaday (left) with John Blair, his successor as director of the New York Zoological Society in 1926. (Photo: Corbis/Bettmann-UPI)

shocking profligacy. In the same decade, new technologies in tanning, plus growing markets for leather in furniture, carriage parts, and machine belts, increased the demand for buffalo hides. Hide hunters armed with repeating rifles boasted killing as many as 120 bison in less than an hour. Thomas Linton, a Kansas buffalo hunter, claimed to have killed more than 3,000 in the 1872 season alone. One half-million buffalo hides were shipped by rail from Dodge City, Kansas, between 1871 and 1874. By 1889, when William Hornaday of the National Museum in Washington, D. C., tried to count the remaining bison population out of what had once been 60 million, he could find only 285 free-ranging animals in the United States.

Easterners who had gone west and witnessed the demise of the buffalo were particularly alarmed. George Bird Grinnell had grown up in Audubon Park, John James Audubon's New York City home, had been tutored by Audubon's widow, and frequented the homes of Audubon's sons, who continued their father's bird study. Trained in paleontology, Grinnell went west in 1870 to collect fossils for Yale's Peabody Museum, and returned again and again over the next ten years. He hunted buffalo with Pawnee Indians, traveled with Buffalo Bill Cody and General George Armstrong Custer, and explored the Black Hills and Yellowstone. Alarmed at the devastation being caused by commercial hunters, afraid that "the large game . . . will 'ere long be exterminated," he wrote articles for *Forest and Stream*, the leading outdoor magazine of its day. In time, he became owner and editor and a leading force for conservation.

Future president Theodore Roosevelt, a bird-watcher since childhood, ranched and hunted in the Dakota badlands in the 1880s, and went on with Grinnell to form the Boone and Crockett Club, a group of influential hunters bent on conserving game and forests. "Conservation of natural resources," he would declare, "is the weightiest problem now before the nation."

While only a few people witnessed the slaughter of the buffalo in the West, many could see the disappearance of birds in the East. In 1876, Joel A. Allen of the American Museum of Natural History noted in

Year-round hunting for sport and especially for the market took a devastating toll of waterfowl and shorebirds until migratory birds came under the federal government's wing in 1918. Before that, hundreds of birds could be killed in a single blast of lead shot from a cannon-like swivel gun mounted on the prow of a punt like this. (Photo: Mystic Seaport, Mystic, Connecticut)

Massachusetts the extermination of the great auk and the wild turkey, the near-extirpation of the whistling swan and the prairie chicken, and greatly reduced numbers of gulls, terns, red-winged blackbirds, crows, red-headed and pileated woodpeckers, wild pigeons, and snow geese. He estimated that waterfowl populations were only a tenth what they had been at the founding of the Massachusetts Bay Colony. "This great diminution," he wrote, "is not limited to the State of Massachusetts, but likewise characterizes most of the Atlantic states." He attributed the decline to clearing of the forests to make farms and to "excess use of the gun."

Reliance upon game for food had created a small army of market hunters. Largely farmers, rural poor, and recent immigrants, they earned seasonal incomes providing robins at five cents a dozen or prairie chickens at fifty cents apiece to hotels, restaurants, and local markets.

With the development of railroads, huge quantities of ducks, prairie hens, and other fowl were shipped long distances to urban markets. This growing commerce took a devastating toll on wildlife. The most tragic example was the passenger pigeon. At the beginning of the nineteenth century, there were perhaps 3 billion passenger pigeons migrating north to nesting grounds in New England and the Great Lakes states. Early settlers commonly described flocks so immense that they blotted out the sun. Some settlers took these passages as omens of impending plague or Indian massacre. But they also provided food so readily that a schoolboy could bring down dozens of pigeons by just throwing sticks into the air. A New Yorker in 1639 reported, "Our people sometimes shoot thirty, forty, and fifty of them at a shot." Early on, settlers shot large numbers, salted them, and packed them into barrels for later use. As the railroads expanded, they shipped the barrels to eastern cities. In 1852, for example, seventy-five tons of pigeons were shipped from New York's Steuben and Allegheny counties alone to New York City.

***Opposite:** With its head feathers erect, and orange throat sacs inflated, a male Attwater's prairie chicken struts for females watching the show on a Texas booming ground. A relative of the greater prairie chicken, this little henlike fowl was once so abundant on the Gulf Coast prairie that marksmen used the birds for target practice. But habitat loss to urbanization, industrial development, and cropland has brought Attwater's prairie chicken to the brink of extinction. Approximately seventy-five of its kind remain in the wild despite the creation of an eponymous national wildlife refuge near Eagle Lake, Texas, on its behalf. (Photo: Tim Fitzharris/Minden Pictures)*

The pigeons were especially vulnerable on their nesting grounds. One could shoot into trees where they roosted, and while hundreds of pigeons fell to the ground, others would stand and wait for the next fusillade. A single hunter with a shotgun and not much skill might easily take a thousand pigeons in a day. Where flocks flew out of the nesting trees to feed, netters would clear the ground and bait it with acorns or corn, then spring nets over the lured pigeons. A skilled netter might take 3,000 birds in one set, then wade in and kill the birds by pinching their skulls between thumb and forefinger. Added to the toll would be the young birds left behind to starve in the nests. The ease of killing drew increasing numbers of hunters: in 1876, when passenger pigeons nested in a 150-square-mile area

near Petoskey, Michigan, they attracted 2,000 hunters, netters, pluckers, and packers.

By the 1880s, the vast flocks of passenger pigeons were gone, and market hunters trained their guns on shorebirds, which also migrated in huge masses. The Eskimo curlew and the golden plover, which flew in flocks of hundreds and sometimes thousands, migrated north through the Mississippi Valley each spring to nesting areas in Canada, and south again sometimes along the New England coast in the fall. A large Eskimo curlew flock was described as being a half a mile long and a hundred yards wide, and Audubon reported a flock of "millions" of golden plovers near New Orleans. One might kill dozens of such birds in a single shot, and often when hunters opened fire, birds would circle over their fallen mates crying in confusion while the hunters fired again and again. Audubon reported 48,000 golden plovers taken in a single hunt, and hunting parties out for a day from Omaha often loaded wagons with Eskimo curlews and still left vast numbers of dead on the ground.

Market hunters would row up to flocks when high tides bunched them on a shoreline, and fire from swivel guns or small cannons, delivering a murderous rain of birdshot. Or the hunters would go out at night with bright lights that blinded and stunned the birds, while hunters waded into the massed birds, clubbing them or wringing their necks. As early as the 1830s, several states outlawed the use of battery guns or night hunting, but there was no enforcement, and the slaughter continued. By 1890, the flocks of Eskimo curlew were gone and the golden plover and other shorebird species were drastically reduced. In 1914, no Eskimo curlews were seen along the New England coast; that same year, the last passenger pigeon died in the Cincinnati Zoo.

Market hunting was not the only cause of decline in wildlife. Sport and sustenance hunters also shot without regard for the survival of game species. It was clear that all forms of hunting should be regulated. But market hunting was more easily seen as excessive because it took such a large toll and because the hunters were willing to destroy the resource for immediate profit, and even sometimes to shoot people who tried to stop them. There was, as well, a class conflict: market hunters were rural folk and recent immigrants, contrasted with men such as Roosevelt and Grinnell, who hunted as a form of leisure. In an age of strong social prejudices, Audubon activists often characterized bird destroyers as those recent immigrants and they called for laws to prohibit them from carrying guns. Market hunters disparaged sport hunters as aristocratic swells who wanted all the game for themselves, and evoked memories of evil European barons in the age of Robin Hood. Replied T. S. Palmer of the Bureau of Biological Survey, "Our game laws, unlike those of Europe, are maintained for the good of the people as a whole, not for the benefit of any one class."

Those game laws were slow to come about. In 1883, Grinnell, Allen, and others brought together

Left: *A museum display of old stuffed birds is a sad substitute for the long-lost sight of millions of passenger pigeons en route to their nesting grounds in the New England and Great Lakes states. Early settlers told of the sun being blotted out by endless streams of pigeons. By 1850, railroad cars loaded with barrels of salted pigeons were being dispatched to eastern cities, and by 1890 there were too few pigeons left to interest market gunners. The last passenger pigeon died in the Cincinnati Zoo in 1914. (Photo: Kjell B. Sandvel/Photo Researchers)*

Opposite: *Seen in full breeding plumage on the Arctic tundra, the golden plover could easily be called the most handsome of all North American shorebirds. Golden plovers were targeted by market hunters on the Great Plains who intercepted the birds' 2,500-mile northbound migration from winter habitat on the Pampas of Argentina. But unlike the passenger pigeon, this boldly marked species managed to hang on and eventually regained some of its historic numbers. (Photo: Art Wolfe)*

***Opposite:** The ruffed grouse is named for the black feathers on its neck, which are erected during spring courtship displays. Fanning his black-bordered tail feathers, the male grouse beats the woodland air with his wings, creating a hollow thumping sound that starts slowly but builds into a drummer's roll. (Photo: Michael Quinton/ Minden Pictures)*

scientists and amateur bird students to form the American Ornithologists' Union (AOU), an organization devoted primarily to improving the scientific understanding of birds. The following year, the AOU established a committee on the protection of birds. Allen and other members of the AOU were convinced that birds were necessary to keep insect pests from putting farmers out of business. In 1884, the AOU appealed to Congress to investigate the agricultural importance of birds, and Congress responded with a $5,000 appropriation and established the Bureau of Biological Survey—forerunner of today's Fish and Wildlife Service—in the U.S. Department of Agriculture. The Bureau's bird studies would do much to show the economic value of birds.

In 1886, Grinnell founded the first Audubon Society, in New York, as "an auxiliary" to the AOU's bird protection committee, hoping concerned citizens would be more effective than the AOU's scientists. In two years the society had 50,000 members, and Grinnell, overwhelmed by the responsibilities, discontinued it to concentrate on *Forest and Stream*. But with the establishment of the Massachusetts Audubon Society in 1896, other states formed Audubon groups and bird protection advanced more rapidly.

The Audubon societies worked on two levels. First, they sought passage of model bird laws in all the states. William Dutcher, first president of the National Association of Audubon Societies, formed in 1905, argued, "If we are to keep the bird it must be by the aid of the law, the only voice that must be listened to, speaking the only language understood by all the races." The AOU had come up with a model law that separated birds into game (ducks, geese, plovers, grouse, sage hens, and others customarily hunted for food) and nongame species (virtually all the rest, though states would leave hawks, owls,

***Right:** Before federal and state laws protected birds of prey—a fairly recent step—it was common to find the carcasses of hawks and owls strung on fences throughout rural America. This scene was photographed in Kentucky in the 1970s and the birds include the great horned owl, red-tailed hawk, and sharp-shinned hawk. (Photo: Karl H. and Stephen Maslowski/Photo Researchers)*

A whimbrel on its way from tundra breeding grounds to far South America stretches a wing during a migration stopover. Because of its large size, the whimbrel has few competitors among other shorebirds for nesting territory and food. And a lone whimbrel like this bird is easy to spot in the company of smaller sandpipers even if its loud whistled cry is not heard. (Photo: Arthur Morris/Birds As Art)

English sparrows, and other species considered to be nuisances unclassified and subject to unrestricted shooting). The law forbade the shooting of nongame species, set bag and season limits for the hunting of game species, and specified fines and penalties for violations. Audubon societies lobbied tirelessly for the laws. New York passed a model law in 1886 and other states followed, one by one, over the next twenty-five years.

What was revolutionary in the AOU model law was that it made birds the domain of the state, denying even a landowner the right to shoot a protected bird on his own property. Some of the early laws softened the blow by including exemptions for farmers finding birds destroying fruit on their land. But it was a challenge to all hunters, who until then regarded hunting as an inalienable right. The new laws made hunting a privilege, with bag limits and season closures set by the state. Acceptance of these new restrictions required a major change in America's view of wildlife.

That led to the Audubon Association's second main focus: education. Mabel Osgood Wright, president of the Connecticut Audubon Society, pointed out that "in the cause of humanity and agricultural economy" women were being asked to give up wearing feathered fashions and men to give up shooting as they pleased, both habits they "regarded as inherent rights." Audubon leaders realized that this change required a reeducation of the public, stressing the values of living birds, first as agricultural amenities because they ate insects, and second as creatures of beauty and abiding interest. "The very least it [the Society] can do," declared Wright, "is to help people become as intimately acquainted with the bird in the

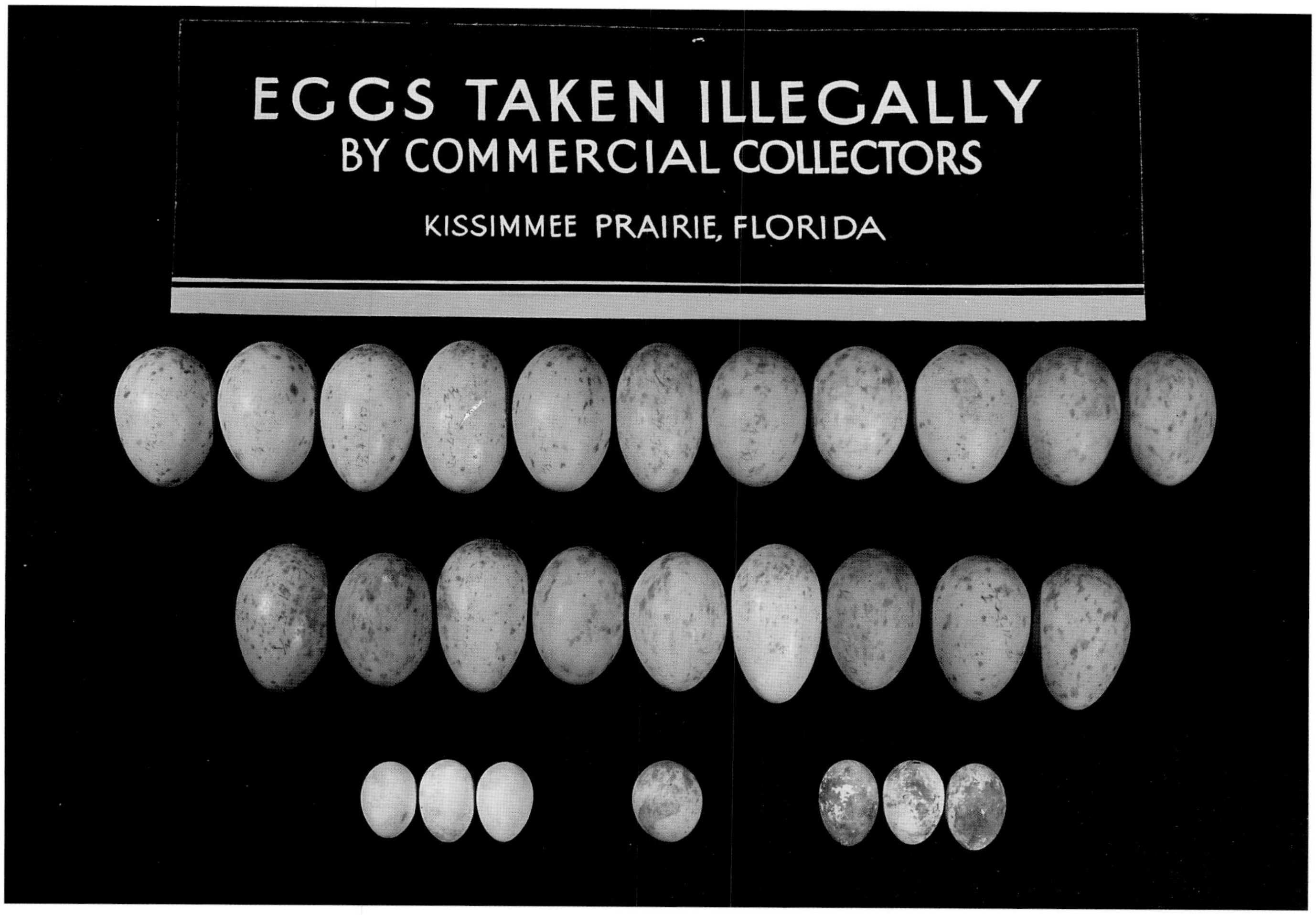
EGGS TAKEN ILLEGALLY
BY COMMERCIAL COLLECTORS
KISSIMMEE PRAIRIE, FLORIDA

So-called oologists—insatiable hobbyists who collected and traded eggs—did immeasurable harm to the breeding success of rare and uncommon birds like Florida's nonmigratory sandhill cranes, represented by the top two rows of large eggs stolen from nests on the Kissimmee Prairie. Egg collecting has been illegal for some years. (Photo: Monroe Carrington/Photo Researchers)

bush as they were with the egg in the pocket and the feather in the hat."

So Audubon societies wrote and published leaflets, species by species, describing the life histories and economic values of birds. They organized Junior Audubon Clubs, teaching birdhouse construction, pledging youths not to kill birds or wear feathers or take eggs, and awarding badges to those who took the pledges. All of this, of course, was aimed at the "creation of a public opinion that would secure legislation in the interest of bird protection, that would spare our birds from threatened extinction."

Women were leaders in the Audubon Association's work, and since they were not usually hunters themselves, spoke less in terms of assuring future supplies of game than in terms of bringing about a higher sense of humanity. This meant—perhaps for all posterity—that the constituency for protecting wildlife would be split between those who valued it as a material resource and those who valued it as a moral and aesthetic resource. The broader terms also led nature writers to attribute human thoughts and motives to animals, a practice Theodore Roosevelt criticized as "nature fakery." Popular nature writer Ernest Thompson Seton, for example, described a crow directing his followers to form a line, and Jack London a she-wolf that "smiled" at the cruelty of her mate. Humanizing animals often increased their appeal, but Frank M. Chapman of the American Museum of Natural History warned Audubon members in 1904 that each should "avoid using his own mind as a standard when attempting to interpret the meaning of an animal's action."

Humane values deepened the emotion and the conviction of bird protectionists, but risked alienating

***Pages 54-55:** A flock of bohemian waxwings in Yellowstone National Park is an unusual sight since these birds of the boreal forest move south only during severe food shortages. Insect eaters during warm months, waxwings rely on berries for sustenance in winter. (Photo: Art Wolfe)*

Although he left school at sixteen and had no scientific training, Frank Chapman became a leading ornithologist, working at the American Museum of Natural History for more than fifty years. Besides his scientific work, he popularized birdwatching among the general public. He founded the Christmas Bird Count, wrote books about conservation, promoted bird photography, encouraged wildlife artists, and founded *Bird-Lore*, which eventually evolved into *Audubon* magazine. Chapman's commitment to conservation led many birdwatchers to become concerned with protecting birds and their habitat.

more materialistic citizens. Wright cautioned that the wider range of argument might cause legislators to distrust Audubon lobbyists and urged, "The goal must be well thought out legislation free from any taint of emotional insanity." In Missouri, in urging the model bird protection law, the Audubon societies launched a study that concluded that "song and insectivorous birds decreased 62 percent and game birds at the appalling rate of nearly 80 percent within the past fifteen years. Deer are practically exterminated. Does any person doubt, unless sweeping reforms are inaugurated at once, that a few years hence will not witness the total annihilation of our birds and game?"

One by one, most of the state legislatures passed some form of bird protection law, asserting state ownership of wildlife. But enforcement was thin at best. Few states employed wardens, and local constables might arrest strangers but wink at neighbors who violated new laws they felt were trivial or outlandish. In 1906, a Texas hunter boasted shooting more than 200 ducks on each of thirty days. A fifteen-year-old South Carolina boy killed thirteen deer in a single day. The Audubon societies had inaugurated a fund with which to pay wardens to watch particularly over rookeries being plundered by plume hunters, and in many states these were the only enforcement officers willing to press charges against illegal hunting.

The model law would not itself suffice to stop market hunting. To accomplish that, Grinnell wrote, "The sale of all game should be forbidden at all seasons." As legislatures were persuaded that market hunting was excessive and that agricultural products could easily and profitably replace game, they gradually restricted the sale of wildlife. But there was no common legal framework; a hunter might shoot protected species and claim to have taken them in a neighboring state, where they weren't protected. Not all states banned the sale of game, so market hunters might shoot in one state and sell in another.

A major step to remedy this discrepancy came with passage in 1900 of the Lacey Act, which made it illegal to ship, receive, or possess game taken illegally to another state and vested enforcement in the Biological Survey. Audubon leaders often used the law to stop commercial hunters. For example, in 1905 J.R. Jack killed ivory-billed woodpeckers in Florida, where the species was presumed extinct, and sent the skins to so-called scientific dealers. Jack eluded prosecution for violating Florida's bird protection law of 1904, declared he knew where more ivory bills were, and added, "I have orders for quite a lot. . . . As soon as I can get off, I expect to go and get all the birds I left." Audubon agents surreptitiously got Jack to send them skins of cardinals and bobwhite quail taken out of season, and successfully had him prosecuted by the Department of Agriculture under the Lacey Act.

With states increasingly adopting model bird laws and season and bag limits, the Lacey Act was a death knell to market hunting; henceforth, game

One chick in her clutch has hatched, but this blue-phase snow goose still has another five or six to go in this down-lined nest near the shore of Hudson Bay. (Photo: Thomas D. Mangelsen)

Young Pacific loons, whose energy needs are several times greater than an adult's, are tended by both parents on the clearwater Arctic lakes where this circumpolar species nests. By one estimate, a pair of loons with two chicks will consume a ton of fish during the fifteen-week breeding season. (Photo: Michael Quinton/ Minden Pictures)

A piping plover incubates a typical four-egg clutch on a Long Island beach. A sparrow-size shorebird the color of sun-bleached sand, the piping plover is listed as a threatened species on the Atlantic Coast because of habitat loss and nest destruction by beach buggies. (Photo: Arthur Morris/Birds As Art)

This female mallard duck is raising goslings from a clutch of Canada goose eggs. When full grown, the young geese will be nearly twice the size of their foster mother. (Photo: Michael Quinton/ Minden Pictures)

would be regarded as a recreational, rather than a commercial resource.

But as soon as the states assumed responsibility for wildlife, competing interests descended on the state legislatures seeking their own special favors. Farmers wanted to declare meadowlarks or robins or other species unprotected. And sport hunters and bird protectionists continually challenged the state bird laws, closing spring hunting one year, reopening it the next. Declared Gilbert Pearson, who succeeded Dutcher as president of the National Association of Audubon Societies, "Bird protection tends to oscillate. The protectionists make a gain one year and then frequently their opponents organize the succeeding years and . . . the pendulum of legislation swings back." In 1908, there were seventy-five bills dealing with bird protection in Connecticut and thirty in Massachusetts. In 1911, nearly 1,000 bills relating to fish and game were offered in the six New England states. Chapman declared, "There is not the slightest doubt that if the Audubon Societies were to disband, in a very few years all of the present excellent bird laws would be so amended that protection would cease."

The desire of sport hunters to continue waterfowl hunting in spring, despite its obvious effect in limiting recovery of a hunted population's numbers, remained a critical issue. The Biological Survey warned, "If any considerable numbers of waterfowl are to be preserved, spring shooting must be abolished." But in many states, sport hunters resisted spring closures. Dutcher declared, "I am afraid we shall never get spring shooting abolished in all the states until we get federal control of our migratory birds."

Audubon leaders worked for a federal law that would bring order to this chaos. In 1904, Pennsylvania Congressman George Shiras III had introduced a bill that declared, "Whereas experience has shown that laws passed by the states and territories of the United States to protect game birds within their respective limits have proved insufficient . . . and the absence of uniform and effective laws and regulations in such cases has resulted in the wholesale destruction and the threatened extermination of many valuable species of said game birds, [all waterfowl, shorebirds, wild pigeons] and other migratory game birds which do not remain permanently the entire year within the borders of any state or territory shall hereafter be deemed to be within the custody and protection of the United States." Opponents charged the law would be an unconstitutional usurpation of state powers, and the bill failed—and did so again when Shiras reintroduced it two years later.

But wildlife protection was gaining public support. After Shiras left Congress, Massachusetts Congressman John W. Weeks reintroduced the bill. This time, at the suggestion of Grinnell, Dutcher, and other wildlife advocates, the terms were broadened to include all migratory birds. The move was in part political strategy, an effort to enlist the support of representatives of farming districts, who were by far the majority in Congress, on the grounds that birds protected crops from insect pests. Pearson called upon Audubon members to "immediately become active and bestir themselves to the point of urging their Senators and Congressmen" to pass the bill. Sportsmen, nature lovers, and farmers united in support, and in 1913 the bill passed.

Chapman crowed in triumph, "The government at Washington has declared that migratory birds are the property of the nation, and not the individual assets of sportsmen, market hunters, game dealers, or millinery collectors . . . and that they shall be protected by federal law."

Almost immediately, the courts disagreed. An Arkansas judge ruled in 1914, "The court is unable to find any provision in the Constitution authorizing Congress, either expressly or by necessary implication,

The female red-necked phalarope is larger and more colorful than her mate, and in a classic case of sex role reversal, it is the male that incubates the eggs and chicks. (Photo: Arthur Morris/Birds As Art)

to protect or regulate the shooting of wild game. . . . The act is unconstitutional." But even before the law had passed, New York Senator and former Secretary of State Elihu Root had suggested that a treaty with Canada, binding the United States government to protect migratory birds, would provide the legal basis by which the federal government might assume responsibility, since under the Constitution a treaty provision supersedes state law. Weeks reintroduced a resolution originally offered by Root authorizing the president to negotiate such a treaty, and it passed quickly. World War I broke out before the exact language of the treaty could be agreed upon and negotiations were stalled, but a treaty emerged in 1916 and the Senate quickly ratified it.

It remained to work out an enabling act to give legal framework to migratory bird protection under the terms of the treaty. In 1918, Congress passed, and President Wilson signed, the Migratory Bird Treaty Act, prohibiting the killing, capture, possession, sale, or shipment of any migratory bird except as provided for by government regulations. It gave the Bureau of Biological Survey power to issue regulations and funds with which to enforce the act.

Chapman declared, "At last migratory birds have been accorded full national citizenship. No longer at the mercy of this state or that, no longer victims of laws made with a view to their destruction rather than protection, they are now wards of the Federal Government."

This time Chapman was right. In succeeding years sportsmen and nonhunters would argue over specific regulations, such as season and bag limits. But the principle had been established that wildlife was the common possession of all, and henceforth bird species would be protected by law.

1920

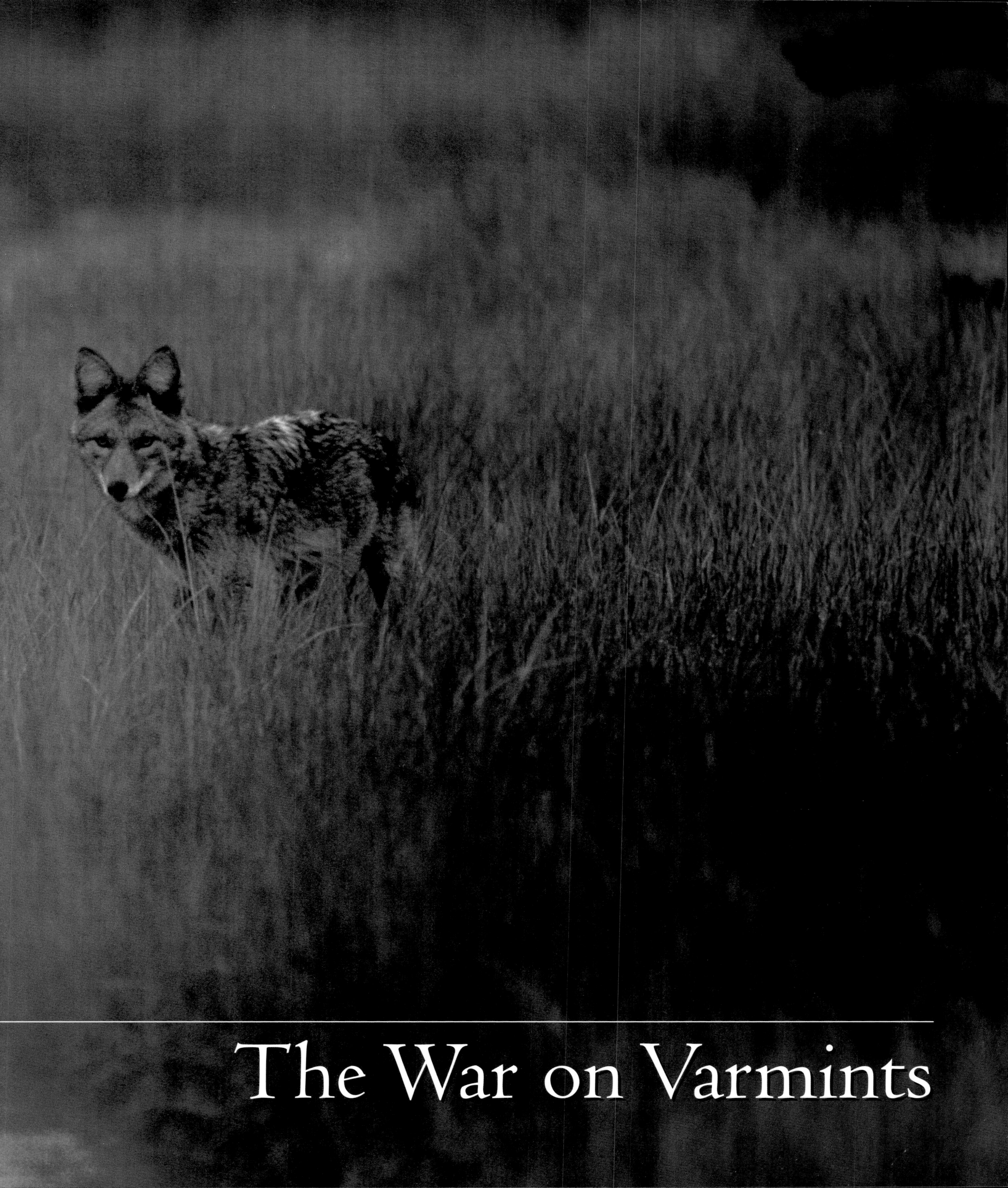

The War on Varmints

1920

The War on Varmints

by Ted Williams

THE WORD *VERMIN*—progenitor of *varmint*—was hatched by gamekeepers on the grouse moors of England. "What isn't game must be vermin," went the dictum. Such attitudes, still prevalent among Europe's landed gentry, migrated to the New World where they eventually were challenged, but not before conservationists found an organized voice. In 1928, for example, the National Association of Audubon Societies (later renamed the National Audubon Society) complained about a British gamekeeper who shot nightingales because, as he said, "They kept the young Pheasants awake!" Another gamekeeper, transported to New York State, was reported by the Association to habitually crush the eggs of vesper sparrows in order to "save food for young Pheasants."

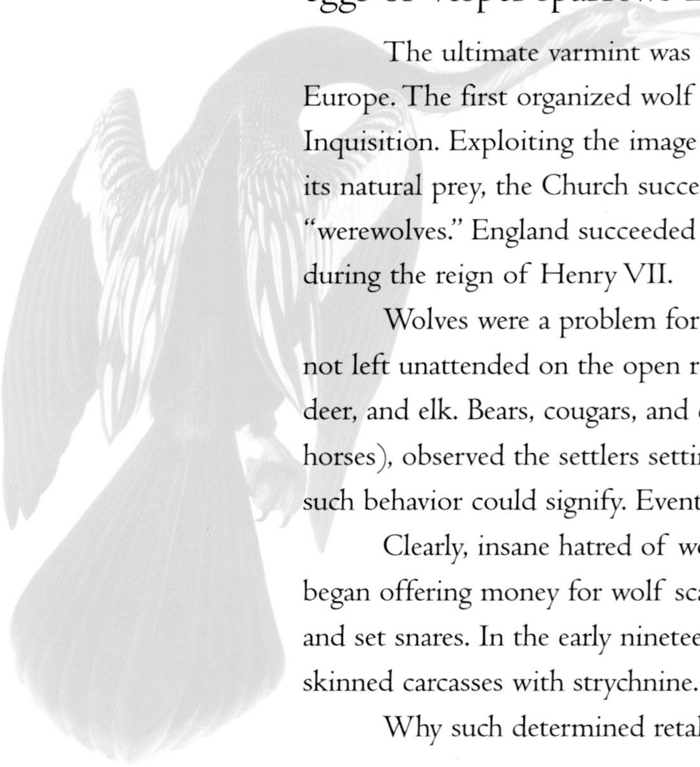

The ultimate varmint was the gray wolf. Again, New World perceptions and superstitions had their origins in Europe. The first organized wolf control, in fact, was sponsored by the Roman Catholic Church during the Inquisition. Exploiting the image of the wolf, which had become a serious stock-killer following the elimination of its natural prey, the Church succeeded in striking fear into the populace by identifying and executing all so-called "werewolves." England succeeded in killing off its last nontransmutable wolf sometime between 1485 and 1509, during the reign of Henry VII.

Wolves were a problem for early American settlers, but not a major one. For one thing, huge herds of stock were not left unattended on the open range. For another, wolves had abundant natural prey in the form of bison, antelope, deer, and elk. Bears, cougars, and coyotes were even less of a threat. When the Indians, who also kept stock (mostly horses), observed the settlers setting out poison bait for predatory mammals, they puzzled long and hard about what such behavior could signify. Eventually they concluded that, among whites, it was a symptom of insanity.

Clearly, insane hatred of wolves is part of our national heritage. In the 1630s, Massachusetts Bay and Virginia began offering money for wolf scalps. Colonists buried fish hooks in balls of meat, dug wolf pits, erected dead falls, and set snares. In the early nineteenth century, professional wolfers shadowed buffalo hunters like vultures, lacing skinned carcasses with strychnine.

Why such determined retaliation? Part of it was Old World baggage and part was loathing of that element of

wild canine behavior which, to humans, appears cowardly and sneaky. When confronted by people, grizzly bears and even black bears and cougars will occasionally attack; wolves will always run away. When trapped or cornered most predators, indeed most animals, will scratch and bite; wolves and coyotes tremble, cower, roll on their backs, and urinate on themselves. The perceived shortcomings of wild canines were well enunciated by Mark Twain in *Roughing It*: "The coyote is a living, breathing allegory of Want. He is always hungry. He is always poor, out of luck, and friendless. The meanest creatures despise him, and even the fleas would desert him for a velocipede [bicycle]. He is so spiritless and cowardly that even while his exposed teeth are pretending a threat, the rest of his face is apologizing for it."

In 1905 the war on wild canines escalated from mechanical and chemical to biological when the Montana Legislature passed a law directing the State Veterinarian to capture wolves and coyotes alive, infect them with mange, and turn them loose.

Despite, or perhaps because of, the prodigious predator-control efforts of states and private citizens, the federal government didn't get seriously into the wolf-control business until 1908 when the U.S. Forest Service reported killing 359 wolves in

Like their domestic cousins, wild coyotes have a playful streak, indulging in mock fights and repeatedly tossing mice into the air until they tire of the game. (Photo: Daniel J. Cox/Natural Exposures)

Pages 60-61: *On a misty autumn morning, a coyote hunts for mice in the deep grass along a Yellowstone creek. When wolves were exterminated in the West, the indomitable coyote became Public Enemy No. 1 in the eyes of ranchers and sportsmen, even though its reputation as a ruthless killer of livestock and game animals such as deer is largely unearned. (Photo: Thomas D. Mangelsen)*

Page 63: *An eight-week-old gray wolf pup nibbles on the ear of its tolerant mother. A sea change in the attitude of most Americans toward wolves led to their successful return to the greater Yellowstone ecosystem in the mid 1990s. (Photo: Art Wolfe)*

Arizona and New Mexico. In 1915 Congress responded to intense lobbying by ranchers and sport hunters with a $125,000 appropriation to the Bureau of Biological Survey. The original mission—killing wolves—quickly expanded to include all predators. In the first year the Survey claimed, probably without much exaggeration, to have accounted for the death of 424 wolves, 9 mountain lions, 11,890 coyotes, and 1,564 bobcats.

Organizing the sportsmen-rancher coalition and leading the anti-predator lobbyists was Aldo Leopold, a passionate and eloquent young forester from New Mexico. "It is well known," Leopold wrote in December 1915, "that predatory animals are continuing to eat the cream off the stock grower's profits. . . . Whatever may have been the value of the work accomplished by bounty systems, poisoning, and trapping, individual or governmental, the fact remains that varmints continue to thrive and their reduction can be accomplished only by means of a practical, vigorous, and comprehensive plan of action. . . . Would not everybody, except the varmints, be benefited by such a move?"

Leopold and his allies weren't content with simple control of offending individuals or even with the trimming of varmint populations. They wanted nothing less than elimination of species. In January 1919, Leopold praised New Mexico for responding to his call and "leading the West in the campaign for eradication of predatory animals. . . . The sportsmen and the stockmen," he declared, "demand the eradication of lions, wolves, coyotes, and bobcats." The following year, addressing the American Game Protective Association in New York City, he proudly announced

The bobcat has three very different hunting techniques. When hunting rabbits or hares, a bobcat will crouch in a "hunting bed" and wait for prey to come hopping along a well-traveled trail. Scurrying rodents are stalked, the bobcat moving as close as possible before a final pounce. Deer are attacked in their beds. (Photo: Tim Fitzharris/ Minden Pictures)

Pages 66-67: *A wolf pack hurdles a snow-banked Montana creek. The stronghold of the wolf in the lower forty-eight states today is not the Rocky Mountain region but the northern Great Lakes states of Minnesota, Wisconsin, and Michigan, along with Isle Royale National Park far out in Lake Superior. (Photo: Daniel J. Cox/Natural Exposures)*

Opposite: *A young raccoon appears to be chinning itself on an aspen branch. Raccoons are omnivorous, welcoming anything edible from snails to garbage, though they are especially fond of crayfish. Raccoons also eat carrion, and uncounted numbers of these innocuous masked bandits were killed when they fed on livestock carcasses laced with strychnine by government predator-control agents. (Photo: Daniel J. Cox/ Natural Exposures)*

Right: *The wolverine is a formidable hunter and its only significant enemy is a trapper, although there are a few accounts of these large members of the weasel clan being killed by wolves. (Photo: Daniel J. Cox/ Natural Exposures)*

that New Mexico had in the last three years knocked down its wolf population from 300 to thirty. Game was now better off, he said, because "the stock industry which covers the entire West is demanding the destruction of predatory animals, and the Bureau of Biological Survey is doing the job rapidly and well." But Leopold warned of the "outstanding need" for the elimination of predators and advised that it was going to be "more difficult and costly to finish the eradication work than it was to start it."

Greatly helping Leopold's cause was the outbreak of rabies in the West and war in Europe. Predators, argued the rancher-sportsman alliance, had to be wiped out in order to preserve public health and save beef for the troops. To tolerate wolves, coyotes, cougars, grizzlies, and the like was to tolerate pestilence and the Hun.

The varmint campaign was expensive both in dollars and incidental casualties. In 1923 the Biological Survey festooned 13 million acres of Arizona with strychnine-laced fat balls which killed—in addition to wolves—ravens, foxes, wolverines, weasels, eagles, dogs, and children. In California, an outraged trapper informed the California Department of Fish and Game that he had found nineteen dead raccoons in Pope's Valley. In another California valley the control of five coyotes entailed an incidental kill of at least 270 striped skunks, then the state's most valuable furbearer.

Still, dread of the gray wolf kept the varmint hunters in business. For ranchers who tended their stock, other predators were nothing more than a minor cost of doing business. Wolves were something else. When the Army, the railroad, and the settlers who came in their wake stripped the plains of bison and antelope, wolves had to choose between starvation or killing livestock. And more than a few ranchers had to choose between going out of business or killing wolves.

By the 1920s the varmint-control bureaucracy found itself confronted with the greatest threat it had faced: America was running out of wolves. "The gray wolf will be exterminated throughout the West within reasonable time," the Biological Survey's J. Stokley Ligon had written in 1918. "The big wolves have been so reduced in numbers in New Mexico and Arizona that they no longer confront us as a serious menace." By 1925 the Survey was able to report that no wolves were rearing young in New Mexico. By the following year it had accounted for the last fourteen wolves in Texas, and its man in Arizona stated that "there are no more wolves left inside the borders of our state." The last wolf was taken from Utah in 1929.

The Survey, however, got a brief reprieve. With the processes of natural selection and behavioral conditioning sped up due to extermination practices, the few wolves that survived possessed astonishing

Opposite, top: The northern Rockies are the grizzly bear's only remaining fortress south of Canada, but a map of the species' historic range includes all the contiguous states from the Great Plains to the Pacific coast. By one estimate, there once were 10,000 grizzlies in California, but by 1924 the last "golden bear," the state's official symbol, had been killed. These grizzlies were photographed in the sanctuary of Alaska's Denali National Park. (Photo: Michio Hoshino/ Minden Pictures)

Opposite, bottom: Ripe elderberries are the attraction of the moment for this striped skunk. Found across North America, this docile black-and-white omnivore is one of the most familiar and most avoided mammals because of the jet of pungent musk it discharges when threatened. Skunks always give ample warning by assuming a defensive posture and stamping their front feet, but dogs in particular rarely get the message. (Photo: Daniel J. Cox/Nature Exposures)

Right: One of the more notorious stock-killing wolves was "Old Three Toes," who had left a digit in the jaws of a trap and led the last wolf pack in the San Juan Mountains of southern Colorado. (Photo: Denver Public Library)

intelligence and seemingly supernatural powers of eluding their human persecutors. Individual wolves—often named for the ways in which they'd been maimed by traps—became national anti-heroes. There was "Old Three Toes," who led the last wolf pack in Colorado, fleeing the San Juan Mountains in 1927 and setting up stock-killing operations in northern New Mexico until blundering into a trap in 1929.

The "Custer Wolf," who terrorized the ranches around Custer, South Dakota, was said to have butchered $25,000 worth of cattle in seven years. "His killings," reported the Biological Survey, "were particularly exasperating, owing to the number of stock slaughtered at times when he appeared to go on a killing debauch, and to the savage mutilation of others—many cows having been killed for the sole purpose of devouring their unborn calves." Legend had it that the Custer Wolf traveled with two coyote sentinels on either flank. Finally the Survey dispatched "one of its best" wolfers, H.P. Williams, who found that the coyote legend was true. Williams shot both sentinel coyotes and in October 1920, after an exhausting six-month chase over 2,600 miles, ended the Custer Wolf's career by trapping him with "scent material obtained from another notorious wolf [also called "Three Toes"] that had been taken by the predatory animal inspector at Split Rock, Wyoming."

In 1921, the Survey assigned Bill Caywood to the seemingly hopeless task of knocking off "Rags the Digger," named for his shaggy coat and *modus operandi* of digging up traps without springing them—seemingly a gesture of contempt that outraged ranchers along the Utah-Colorado border country. Caywood, who had been ridding the West of wolves

Pages 72-73: This Minnesota red fox in its plush winter coat will consume five pounds of food in a week, mainly mice and rabbits. In the wild canine hierarchy, coyotes cannot compete with wolves, and in turn they do not tolerate the presence of foxes. (Photo: Tim Fitzharris/ Minden Pictures)

Pronghorns, distinctly North American and not allied to Old-World goats or antelope, are the fastest land mammals on earth after cheetahs. In the 1830s they may have outnumbered even bison, stretching in vast herds from California to Minnesota, from southern Canada to Mexico. But then came plows, cows, sheep, and commercial hunters, and by 1915 pronghorns were down to fewer than 15,000.

Recovery of this prized big-game trophy was effected accidentally by a decline in the sheep industry, and on purpose by controls on the grazing of competing livestock, the banning of market hunting, and enlightened sport–hunting regulations. Today there are about one million pronghorns in the West, and the population is stable.

—Ted Williams

Male pronghorns face off in South Dakota's Wind Cave National Park. (Photo: Jim Brandenburg/Minden Pictures)

for thirty years, was said by the *Rocky Mountain News* to be "the greatest Colorado wolfer of all time," as well as "a friend to all animals and regretful executioner of those outlaws who must die that other wild creatures and domestic animals may live."

The panic spread by the "super wolves" made the Survey's work appear essential, but even they were vanishing from the West. Now it was the varmint control bureaucracy that faced two hard choices: go out of business or convince the public that there was more work for it to do in the form of ridding the nation of "vermin" as defined in England: everything that isn't game. The agency took to lobbying and advertising. For example, the 1920 Yearbook of the Department of Agriculture contained a fire-and-brimstone sermon, replete with wild, utterly unsubstantiated statistics, entitled "Hunting Down Stock Killers," in which its own W.B. Bell wrote: "Uncle Sam, tired of the drain on his resources of from $20,000,000 to $30,000,000 every year through the slaughter of domestic stock by predatory animals, now keeps constantly in the field a force of hunters who are instructed to wipe out these non-producers. . . . Statistics may leave the stockman unmoved and uninterested, but a vivid, lasting impression is made when he finds . . . one of his colts struck down by a mountain lion, the scattered carcasses of several of his sheep killed by coyotes for sheer lust of killing, or a valuable cow maimed or with skull crushed by a blow from the powerful paw of a grizzly." Of the rabies outbreak—a natural and cyclical phenomenon—Bell wrote: "Driven by their rabid blindness, coyotes entered the yards of dwellings, attacking dogs, cats, human occupants, or any object they might

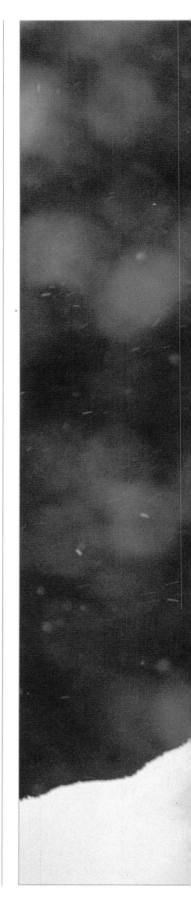

Opposite: *The blacktail prairie dog is a plump ground squirrel whose "ravages and depredations discourage settlement and in many cases drive out settlers," according to an old bulletin from the U.S. Department of Agriculture. Government agents continue to spread lethal chemicals in prairie dog towns even though scientists tell us the social rodent is a "keystone species" on which 170 animals depend to one degree or another, among them the mountain plover and swift fox, both vanishing species. (Photo: Tom Bean)*

Right, top: *Then and now, hunters have used dogs to tree mountain lions. Even the National Park Service had a policy in its early decades calling for the extermination of the wolf, coyote, lion, fox, lynx, bobcat, wolverine, fisher, badger, mink, and other "predator" species. (Photo: Denver Public Library)*

Right, bottom: *Dick Randall was a federal predator control agent when he displayed a coyote pelt and a large bobcat for a photographer in 1969. Randall subsequently was reborn as a humane activist and went to work for Defenders of Wildlife, trading his traps for a camera. (Photo: Defenders of Wildlife)*

Pages 76-77: *Painted turtles catch the sun in Minnesota's Boundary Waters Canoe Area Wilderness. A waterfowl sanctuary in Michigan reported killing more than 5,000 turtles in a five-year period. (Photo: Jim Brandenburg/Minden Pictures)*

Page 77, top: *Even the desert roadrunner found its way onto predator-control lists, probably because it sometimes eats the eggs of small birds in addition to scorpions, lizards, snakes, and rodents. (Photo: Tim Fitzharris/Minden Pictures)*

Page 77, bottom: *In the 1920s, National Park Service rangers patrolled the white pelican breeding colonies on Yellowstone Lake, crushing the eggs because the birds ate cutthroat trout. (Photo: Jim Brandenburg/Minden Pictures)*

encounter; they entered feed lots and snapped and infected cattle, sheep, and other domestic animals; and also attacked pedestrians, horsemen, and automobiles on public highways."

In 1928, Survey chief Paul G. Redington warned Congress and the public that his agency "faced the opposition . . . of those who want to see the mountain lion, the wolf, the coyote, and the bobcat perpetuated as part of the wildlife of the country."

Prairie dogs provided another opportunity to expand the varmint extermination programs. Because these heavy-bodied ground squirrels do best on denuded landscapes where they can spot predators at long distances, they were one of the few species that proliferated with cows. There was—and is—no scientific evidence that prairie dogs reduce the amount of forage available to cattle on well-managed range; and there is considerable evidence that they increase it by aerating and turning over soil. But the Biological Survey proclaimed that prairie dogs were a menace to ranching and set about poisoning them on a grand scale with zinc phosphate and strychnine. From 1919 to 1922 it claimed to have killed five million in Arizona alone. Stockmen, it said, "are adding to their flocks and herds as forage for additional animals is provided by the eradication of such range-destroying rodents as prairie dogs, ground squirrels, and related pests." In 1928, the Survey switched to the far more lethal and nonselective poison, thallium sulfate. The following year the varmint controllers got new status when the Survey's Division of Ornithology and Mammalogy was renamed the Division of Predatory Animal and Rodent Control.

It is impossible to determine to what extent the Survey influenced public attitudes or reflected them. In any case, the 1920s saw a ravaging of every species that ate, might eat, or looked hungrily at a species humans wanted to eat first. There was, for example, anhinga control, road-runner control, hawk

control, eagle control, crow control, blue-jay control, kingfisher control, loon control, even painted-turtle control. From 1927, when it was founded, until July 1931, the W. K. Kellogg Bird Sanctuary near Battle Creek, Michigan, reported destroying 2,298 snapping turtles and 2,688 "other turtles."

Between 1925 and 1930 Maryland paid bounties on 89,858 hawks. It repealed the bounty in 1931, not because it was getting soft on hawks but because it couldn't collect enough revenue from hunting licenses to pay the half-dollar for each carcass. At the same session the Maryland Legislature removed protection for bald eagles. Ohio repealed its hawk bounty in 1933, but then distributed free hawk ammunition so that the kill rose from 2,022 in 1932 to 4,003 in 1934.

In 1924, the National Park Service looked upon white pelicans and determined that they were bad. Not only did they eat cutthroat trout, they served as hosts for the tapeworms with which both species had coexisted for millennia. Each spring, rangers patrolled pelican breeding colonies on Yellowstone Lake's Molly Islands, carefully crushing eggs. In 1931, the year pelican control ended in the park, a particularly dedicated scientist named Lowell Woodbury set up an experiment to determine if cutthroat-pelican tapeworms could survive in mammalian digestive tracts. Accordingly, he swallowed fourteen live ones, sucking them down like spaghetti. All the tapeworms perished.

Raptor control was aggressively pushed by sportsmen and conservationists alike. William Hornaday, a founder of the American Bison Society, conceiver and first superintendent of the National Zoological Park in Washington, D.C., and author of the influential 1913 book *Our Vanishing Wild Life,* advocated elimination of horned, barred, and screech owls; goshawks, Cooper's and sharp-shinned hawks; and golden eagles and peregrine falcons. As a champion of waterfowl he nursed a special hatred for this last varmint, alias "duck hawk," of which he wrote: "Each

bird of this species deserves treatment with a choke bore gun. First shoot the male and female, then collect the nest, the young or the eggs, whichever may be present. They all look best in collections."

In the 1920s Hornaday enthusiastically reported that a boy named Willie Hall of Watson, Saskatchewan,

Birdwatchers on the crest of Pennsylvania's Blue Mountain scan the sky for migrating hawks. Sport hunters armed with shotguns slaughtered huge numbers of birds of prey from this vantage point until Hawk Mountain Sanctuary was created in 1932. (Photo: Jerry Irwin/Photo Researchers)

had won a provincial competition by collecting 1,445 eggs and 5,216 legs of crows and magpies. Totals for all competitors were 696,201 eggs and 239,901 legs. "In the face of these figures," Hornaday commented, "there can be no doubt about the necessity of eliminating a lot of those superfluous birds."

Gradually, however, Americans learned that nothing in nature is "superfluous." What is remarkable is not that they engaged in European-style "vermin" control but that they repudiated it so quickly. Part of the reason may be that in the United States it is more difficult for one special interest to determine how wildlife will be managed because game and nongame are owned by the public instead of by landed gentry.

As early as 1920, Yellowstone National Park was arguing against Aldo Leopold's vision of extermination, despite the fact that it destroyed 107 coyotes and 28 wolves that year: "It is hardly practicable, even if it were desirable, to entirely exterminate these animals." In 1931 the National Park Service banned poisons except for rodents, and the same year director Horace Albright issued this landmark policy statement: "Predatory animals are to be considered an integral part of the wild life protected in national parks, and no widespread campaigns of destruction are to be countenanced. The only control practice is that of shooting coyotes and other predators when they are actually found making inroads upon herds of game or other animals needing special protection." By 1936 the Park Service was calling for the reintroduction of "any native species which had been exterminated" from a national park.

Members of the American Society of Mammalogists began calling federal varmint controllers "gopher-chokers." At the Society's 1924 annual meeting, speakers attacked the Biological Survey's policy of exterminating species and charged that it had abandoned science in order to appease ranchers. "There is little doubt," remarked Milton Skinner, a former Yellowstone ranger and chief naturalist, "that [wolves] played their part in developing speed and cunning among many forms of animals and in preventing epidemics" by preying upon older, weaker, or infirm animals.

Top, right: Under Director Horace Albright (right), the National Park Service changed its policy toward predators in the early 1930s and called for the reintroduction of any species which had been exterminated. But it took sixty years before wolves were returned to Yellowstone, where Albright poses at a ceremony marking the park's golden anniversary. (Photo: Corbis/Bettmann/UPI)

Bottom, right: Aldo Leopold inspects a white pine on his Wisconsin River farm. Early in his career as a forester, Leopold was an advocate of predator control but in 1944 he was the first to call for restoring wolves to Yellowstone National Park. (Photo Courtesy the State Historical Society of Wisconsin)

Pages 80-81: A meadow of *Helianthella* or aspen sunflowers in the Aldo Leopold Wilderness of New Mexico. Smaller and paler than the true sunflower, this composite blooms in aspen groves in June but is also encountered at timberline. (Photo: David Muench)

Such comments drew fiery responses like this one from the Survey's E. A. Goldman: "Large predatory mammals, destructive to livestock and game, no longer have a place in our advancing civilization."

But the mammalogists kept protesting. Especially passionate was A. Brazier Howell of Johns Hopkins Medical School, who circulated a petition among august scientific institutions calling nonselective federal varmint control a danger to the "very existence of all carnivorous mammals." Signatories included the California Academy of Sciences, Field Museum of National History in Chicago, American Museum of Natural History in New York, San Diego Natural History Society, and Academy of Natural Sciences in Philadelphia. The indefatigable Howell even sounded off in *Outdoor Life* magazine: "Ten to twenty years ago there was frequent reference in Biological Survey literature to the immense amount of benefit, through destruction of rodents, that the coyote, badger, *et al.* conferred upon the farmer. Recently there is no slightest reference to such benefit to be encountered in Survey publications, but only the misdeeds of these 'pests.'"

"No longer is the game hog the chief threat to our fauna," announced Howell at the Society of Mammalogists' 1930 meeting, "but rather the pseudo-conservationist who agitates for the protection of one or two game species and the eradication of everything else." At the same meeting, Charles C. Adams, of the New York State Museum, gleefully quoted Survey pronouncements on the evils of predators, drawing gales of laughter from the audience. With that, the group appointed a varmint-control study committee which, in due course, recommended that the Society resolve to "deplore the propaganda of the survey which is designed to unduly blacken the character of certain species of predatory mammals, giving only part of the facts and withholding the rest."

The most eloquent proponent of predator eradication eventually became its most eloquent critic. Aldo Leopold, the New Mexico forester who in 1915 had led anti-predator lobbyists, had reversed his original position. From the board of the National Association of Audubon Societies and

In 1948 Aldo Leopold suffered a fatal heart attack while fighting a fire on his Wisconsin pine plantation. His most enduring work, *A Sand County Almanac*, had not yet been published, but Leopold, a renowned game-management specialist and former Forest Service forester, had already distinguished himself as an environmental pioneer. He had been trained at the Yale Forest School in the utilitarian principles of Gifford Pinchot-style conservation, but in an article in the November 1921 *Journal of Forestry*, he startled his colleagues by questioning the traditional notion that "the policy of development . . . should continue to govern in absolutely every instance." Wasn't it possible, he asked, that "the principle of highest use" demanded that "representative portions of some forests be preserved as wilderness?"

In 1924, when Leopold was stationed in New Mexico, he persuaded his superiors to designate 500,000 acres of the state's national-forest land as the Gila Wilderness, the first designated wilderness area in American history. In 1935 he and Robert Marshall founded the Wilderness Society, which was instrumental in the passage of the Wilderness Act of 1964 and in the subsequent growth of the national wilderness system to more than 104 million acres. Still, it is *A Sand County Almanac*, published in 1949, that gives Leopold immortality. An essay called "The Land Ethic," which is grafted onto a collection of artful and often wise seasonal observations, contains the philosophical heart of twentieth-century environmentalism.

Its thesis, like most great ideas, is simply stated: "All ethics so far evolved rest upon a single premise: that the individual is a member of a community of interdependent parts. . . . The land ethic simply enlarges the boundaries of community to include soils, waters, plants, and animals, or collectively: the land. . . . In short, a land ethic changes the role of *Homo sapiens* from that of the land community to plain member and citizen of it." These words made Leopold's book a sacred text, at least for a movement hoping to achieve a moral universe that includes the needs of the land in its system of values.

—T. H. Watkins

from the chair in game management created for him at the University of Wisconsin, Leopold—the forester turned ecologist—scolded his former allies. "When we attempt to say an animal is 'useful,' 'ugly,' or 'cruel,' we are failing to see it as part of the land," he declared. "We do not make the same error of calling a carburetor 'greedy.'" In 1944 he was to call for wolf restoration in Yellowstone. And in 1947, as part of *A Sand County Almanac*'s foreword that was deleted from the published version, he wrote: "In 'Escudilla,' I relate my own participation in the extinguishment of the grizzly bear from the White Mountain region. At the time I sensed only a vague uneasiness about the ethics of this action. It required the unfolding of official 'predator control' through two decades finally to convince me that I had helped to extirpate the grizzly from the Southwest, and thus played the role of accessory in an ecological murder."

The 1930 admonishments of the American Society of Mammalogists almost convinced Congress to cancel the Division of Predatory Animal and Rodent Control's annual $1 million appropriation. But in a last-minute compromise, PARC agreed to get a new chief and reduce its program. Then the livestock

Beginning in the mid-1920s, the National Audubon Society urged protection for birds of prey like the great horned owl (left) and Cooper's hawk. But it took nearly half a century before the public image of hawks and owls was significantly changed. (Photos: Ron Austing; Tim Fitzharris/ Minden Pictures)

lobby went to work, and the next year Congress passed the Animal Damage Control Act, which provided the first clear authority for federal varmint control and institutionalized it as a government service.

The lay sector was slower to respond to the war against varmints. But under the leadership of the National Association of Audubon Societies, it eventually made itself heard, particularly on the persecution of birds of prey, or raptors. During the 1920s, the Association never quite managed to grasp the concept that no native species can be ecologically "destructive." But in its bimonthly magazine, *Bird-Lore*, one can see it struggling with conventional wisdom.

"Let us recognize frankly [a predator's] existence," it exhorted members in July 1926. "Let us admire whatever of beauty and interest there is in it, but let us not hinder its control when that is necessary." From January 29 to February 5, 1927, the Association sponsored a raptor display at the New England Sportsmen's Show in Boston, urging protection for "useful Hawks and Owls" but also including "the relatively few species which in their feeding habits destroy such a quantity of smaller species of both song- and game-birds as to warrant the human responsibility of controlling their numbers." By 1930 the model "Audubon law," as it was called, had been enacted in about forty states. It extended protection to all birds of prey except the Cooper's hawk, goshawk, sharp-shinned hawk, and the great horned owl.

Ultimately, the Association grew uncomfortable with the persecution of any species. It published accounts of how great horned owls had been converted to "loving pets" and interviewed such alleged vermin as kingfishers, one of which eruditely excuses himself as follows: "I know I am blamed for the poor fishing in this stream, and I will admit that I occasionally get a little trout, but if you want to see who really gets the fish, come out here on Saturday or Sunday."

Sheep ranchers from Wyoming to Texas stepped up their campaign against the magnificent golden eagle—a protected species—in the late 1970s, hiring helicopters as shooting platforms for varmint hunters. Nearly 800 golden as well as bald eagles were shot from one pilot's aircraft. (Photo: Konrad Wothe/Minden Pictures)

In 1930 the Association got a bald-eagle protection bill through both houses of Congress, but in the Senate livestock interests wangled an exception for birds caught in the act of destroying "domestic fowl, wild or tame lambs or fawns or foxes on fox-farms."

Two years later the Association stepped up its crusade against the slaughter of hawks by sport hunters, reporting that at Pennsylvania's Blue Mountain 218 birds had been picked up in about an hour following a Sunday shoot, and that no effort was made to avoid hitting "beneficial" species. "When 100 to 150 men, armed with pumpguns, automatics, and doubled-barreled shotguns are sitting on top of a mountain looking for a target, no bird's safe." Two years later Blue Mountain became the world's first raptor sanctuary.

Even as America began to grasp the basic principles of ecology, backwaters of superstition lingered. For example, bald eagles did not receive meaningful federal protection until 1940, golden eagles not until 1962. As recently as 1971, helicopter pilot James O. Vogan testified before a Senate subcommittee that he had been illegally retained by local sheep ranchers to provide an airborne gun platform for varmint hunters in Colorado and Wyoming. According to his records, they'd dispatched 770 bald and golden eagles from his aircraft alone. "With some shooters," said Vogan, "I'd have to tell them when to shoot. Others, one kid, just knew. I'd line 'em up and they would fire . . . We'd get fifty or sixty on a good day."

It has been a slow, agonizing process, but most of the public, the game management establishment, and, to a large extent, even the livestock industry have learned that the non-selective elimination of varmints at the very best accomplishes nothing.

Now that Yellowstone National Park protects

Once believed to be extinct, the black-footed ferret maintains a tenuous presence in the West through releases of captive-raised animals at a cost of $5,000 each. However, experts doubt there will ever be enough ferrets and their prairie dog prey to maintain self-sustaining wild populations. (Photo: Jim Brandenburg/ Minden Pictures)

both white pelicans and cutthroat trout, the former annually consume 300,000 pounds of the latter. Both are well endowed with tapeworms, and there are far more of all three species than in the 1920s. In 1946 gopher-chokers killed 294,000 coyotes in seventeen western states. In 1974, after twenty-eight years of indiscriminate trapping, shooting, denning, and poisoning, they killed 295,000 coyotes in the same seventeen states. During this period coyotes expanded their range, populating the East.

As the Biological Survey demonstrated, it is possible to denude the landscape of wolves. But the wolf, never a major predator of sheep, is the only coyote control that ever worked. And the coyote, in turn, is the only fox control that ever worked. Following an all-out air and ground campaign against coyotes in the prairie-pothole region in the 1930s, the fox population erupted. The coyotes had not been a major predator of waterfowl. But foxes are a duck's worst nightmare. They patrol much smaller territories, so there are more of them to raid nests and, unlike coyotes, they don't stop when they're full because they cache eggs.

There are still battles to be fought. Today the leadership of the Alaska Department of Fish and Game devoutly believes that predator control is the key to game abundance. In 1992, then Governor Wally Hickel defended the department's "management" of wolves—gunning them down from aircraft—with this pronouncement to the press: "You just can't let nature run wild." In January 1993, he hosted a "Wolf Summit" in Fairbanks at which Fish and Game officials tried vainly to educate wolf advocates from out of state. "We feel we are going to create a wildlife spectacle [the annual caribou migrations] on a par with the major [wildebeest] migrations in East Africa," effused Wildlife Director David "Machinegun" Kelleyhouse (so called because he had tried to requisition a fully automatic weapon for his management work). More recently the department has been pushing the politically correct but no less ecologically hurtful practice of wolf sterilization.

The war on prairie dogs nearly caused the extinction of the black-footed ferret—which depends on them for food and habitat. In 1979 the ferret was presumed extinct after the last survivor of a South Dakota colony had died in captivity. But two years later a ranch mutt named Shep killed a ferret near Meeteetse, Wyoming. When state biologists attempted to save the ferrets from distemper and sylvatic plague (an alien pathogen from Europe) by evacuating the wild stock, the species seemed doomed. *Audubon* magazine even published an opinion piece entitled "The Final Ferret Fiasco." But today the Fish and Wildlife Service has a captive breeding population of some 400 animals. And it has released almost a thousand in Montana, Wyoming, South Dakota, Utah, Arizona, and Colorado.

The future, however, is not bright for the black-footed ferret. Not only are prairie dogs beset by sylvatic plague, but the private and federal poison war continues. Perhaps the prevailing attitude toward prairie dogs in the West is best expressed by the International Varmint Association (IVA), which lobbies against the poisoning of prairie dogs so that there will be more of them to blow away with high-powered rifles. IVA seeks "IVG," that is, the "Instant Visual Gratification" of being "able to actually see the bullet strike its mark and watch the target disintegrate in the scope." Essential to IVG is the cloud of blood that hangs in the air after the bullet blows apart a prairie dog. Some members wear T-shirts that say "Red Mist Society."

In mainstream society, however, the persecution of varmints has not been socially acceptable at least since the 1970s. So the varmint-control bureaucracy is forever changing its name. "Predatory Animal and Rodent Control" became "Wildlife Services," which became "Animal Damage Control" (ADC). But in 1989, brainstorming sessions between ADC and the U.S. Fish and Wildlife Service spawned a report with this suggestion: "Start using the term Animal Damage Management (ADM) instead of Animal Damage Control (ADC), unless it is in reference to an Act or agency." After a consultant

Right: *The handsome blue jay was once persecuted because it sometimes robs the nests of other songbirds. (Photo: Richard Day/Daybreak Imagery)*

advised that "Animal Damage Control" contained three negative words, the agency changed its name back to "Wildlife Services."

But no matter what the gopher-chokers call themselves they still don't get any respect. And that's unfortunate because the alternative to professional gopher-choking is vigilantism; and while the pros don't always do it right, vigilantes usually do it wrong. The environmental community tends not to recognize this. When their publications run articles on the activities of Wildlife Services, they invariably dig up forty-year-old photos of animals trapped, burned, and poisoned by federal gopher-choker Dick Randall who, born again as a humane activist, went to work for Defenders of Wildlife.

Wildlife Services still kills plenty of coyotes and other animals, so that the public gets to pay three times for the privilege of hosting private livestock on its rangeland—once with its tax money, once with its predators, and once with habitat damage by domestic ungulates. But at least today's predator control is relatively selective. Much of the work is essential (gull

Page 86: *The northern raven's croaking call is a familiar sound in mountain forests and along wild seascapes. (Photo: Thomas D. Mangelsen)*

Pages 86-87: *A bald eagle strikes a regal pose in the Tongass rain forest of southeast Alaska. (Photo: Art Wolfe)*

control at airports, for example) and more than half is nonlethal. For example, the agency's National Wildlife Research Center at Fort Collins, Colorado, (formerly called the "Eradication Methods Laboratory"), has induced ravens to avoid one of their favorite repasts—the eggs of the endangered California least tern—by injecting quail eggs with methiocarb, a substance that makes birds throw up. When the dosed quail eggs are placed in least tern nests, the ravens associate their sickness with tern eggs and decide they hate tern eggs, too.

Wildlife Services says it would like to get seriously into control of the cowbird, a woodland-bird scourge that has been thriving with forest fragmentation. But the bird-control staffers can't get any constituents. The environmental community won't talk to them because they are the enemy.

Despite such blinders from the varmint wars, the environmental community has made remarkable progress in dragging the nation toward what Leopold called an "ecological conscience." In 1974, when gray wolves were declared endangered in the Rocky Mountains, recovery seemed politically impossible. And the climate seemed no better in the late 1980s when U.S. Fish and Wildlife Service director Frank Dunkle assured the Wyoming Wool Growers Association that the only wolves he'd bring to Yellowstone were on his tie tack. Yet in the winter of 1995, Fish and Wildlife Service director Mollie Beattie and her boss, Interior Secretary Bruce Babbitt—both spewing quotes from the reformed Leopold—carried wolves captured in Canada into the park. The recovery plan, written in 1987, called for ten breeding pairs in each of three areas: northwest Montana, the greater Yellowstone ecosystem, and central Idaho. By 1998, that goal essentially had been attained.

Environmentalists still get discouraged about public attitudes toward "varmints," occasionally with excellent reason. But for the melancholic, there is simple therapy: Visit a known hawk lookout—maybe Blue Mountain (now called Hawk Mountain) in Kempton, Pennsylvania—on a clear September morning with thermals building and a wind out of the northwest. Stare at the forest of spotting scopes. Listen to the banter of bird-club leaders as they converse by two-way radio with leaders on lookouts to the north and south. "Crackle, crackle . . . three ospreys and a bald eagle heading your way."

Now envision a resurrected Hornaday in derby cap, wool shirt, and suspenders. He pushes through the crowd, curtly explaining that he is here "that other wild creatures and domestic animals may live." He raises his 12-gauge autoloader, clicks off the safety, crumples a passing peregrine, then fires the remaining four rounds into a kettle of broadwings.

Now imagine his reception and his fate.

1930

Gaining Ground

1930

Gaining Ground

by Peter Steinhart

OAKLAND, CALIFORNIA'S, LAKE MERRITT claims distinction as the nation's first public wildlife refuge. In 1870, prodded by Oakland mayor, Samuel Merritt, who felt careless waterfowl hunters reduced the value of properties he was developing on the lakeshore, just outside the city limits, the California legislature banned hunting there. No land was set aside, and much of the diked-off San Francisco Bay slough was filled to build a courthouse, a municipal auditorium, and a county museum. Today 160-acre Lake Merritt is a downtown city park, and the cackle of Canada geese and the quack of mallards mix with the rush of traffic echoing off high-rise apartments and office buildings. The park hosts two boathouses, a lawn bowling complex, a children's amusement park, a children's art and science center, a sprawling garden club facility, and a nature center.

In 1915, after an oil spill killed legions of ducks, the city passed an ordinance pledging in perpetuity to feed the birds in the refuge. Every day at 3:30, spectators watch the nature center staff toss millet seed for the ducks and chunks of fish for pelicans and egrets. Pigeons crowd the feeding area, racing the ducks for grain. For ten years the same brown pelican has performed a crowd-pleasing dance for the handouts.

In 1927, the National Association of Audubon Societies' publication, *Bird-Lore,* viewed Lake Merritt as an ideal bird sanctuary. In the 1930s our ideas of refuges changed, and what once was viewed as a model refuge is today seen as little more than a small zoo. The first stirrings of wildlife conservation sought only to change hunting habits. At the turn of the century the idea of a refuge was new and vaguely defined. A number of towns had ordinances outlawing shooting—probably as much for public safety as to spare the lives of birds. A number of private landowners declared their property bird refuges by posting "no hunting" signs and prosecuting those who disobeyed as trespassers. There was little effort to manage the habitat to protect wildlife or to defend it from development.

Those who feared, as did Madison Grant of the Boone and Crockett Club, that "Twenty-five years hence, game in North America in a wild state will almost have ceased to exist," urged the establishment of zoos to preserve specimens of wild animals for study and possible later restocking. The Boone and Crockett Club campaigned successfully

Lake Merritt in Oakland, California, was America's first public wildlife refuge. Now a downtown park with a population of tame mallards and Canada geese, the former San Francisco Bay slough was closed to waterfowl hunting by the state legislature to protect the value of lakeside property being developed by the city's mayor. (Photo: David Weintraub/Photo Researchers)

for the establishment, in 1895, of the New York Zoological Park, and Grant became its first president.

By 1900, conservationists were considering the idea of a preserve, modeled vaguely after the game preserves of European royalty, but without the aristocratic aims. Willard Van Name, a Yale University biologist, writing in Audubon's *Bird-Lore*, urged, "A few preserves comprising some of the marshes or beaches along the coast, or some of the ponds or swamps in inland districts, which could furnish safe resorts and feeding grounds for the various water birds during the migrations and during the breeding season for such as would remain and breed, would help to preserve the birds which the state game laws have never properly cared for, and would induce the birds to visit regions which they have to a great extent deserted on account of the constant persecution they suffer."

Mabel Osgood Wright, President of the Connecticut Audubon Society, compared preserves to the reservations assigned to conquered Indian tribes. "Now that civilization is reducing the woodlands and wild tracts that for ages have been the birds' hunting grounds, should not they too be provided with suitable reservations, where the food natural to such places shall be sufficiently supplemented and the supply placed beyond the vicissitudes of weather?" A few small examples existed, such as the Hampton Preserve at Windham, Connecticut, begun in 1894 when E. Knight Sperry got a half-dozen private landowners to put up "No Hunting" signs, stock the land with quail, and let patches of wheat and buckwheat go to seed to provide cover for the birds.

The perception was dawning, as wildlife biologist Aldo Leopold would write in the 1940s, "that game, to be successfully conserved, must be positively produced, rather than negatively protected." In 1891, when the first national forest was established to protect watersheds, it was thought that hunters would be kept out simply to prevent forest fires. George Bird Grinnell—editor of the leading outdoor magazine of the time, *Forest and Stream*—saw such areas as "the nurseries and breeding grounds for game and the large wild animals which are elsewhere inevitably exterminated by the march of settlement." However, in the West where most of the forests were being set aside, ranchers, miners, and hunters were incensed at the closures, and after Theodore Roosevelt became president in 1901, his chief forester, Gifford Pinchot, sought to have only small parts of each forest declared off-limits to hunting.

It would prove easier to set aside refuges for birds than for deer or elk because birds—especially communally nesting species like gulls, terns, herons, and egrets—required less space and because there was growing public support for protecting birds from market hunters.

In 1903, the National Association of Audubon Societies sought to protect from plume-hunters the pelican colony on a four-acre island in Florida's Indian River. The Audubon Association's president, William

Pages 88-89: The bantam deer of the Florida Keys stand about two feet tall at the shoulders and are the smallest race of the familiar white-tailed deer. Bucks scale 55 to 75 pounds, does are smaller, and newborn fawns are no larger than a puppy. By comparison, an average buck in the North Woods of Michigan might weigh 200 pounds. Once seen throughout the Lower Keys, the little deer was hunted to near extinction. Only twenty-six survivors were found in 1949, when the Boone and Crockett Club hired a full-time warden, armed with a Tommygun, to ward off poachers until a Key Deer National Wildlife Refuge could be created. (Photo: Daniel J. Cox/Natural Exposures)

Page 90: President Theodore Roosevelt created the first federal bird refuge in 1903 to protect a crowded colony of brown pelicans on Florida's east coast—Pelican Island. At the time, Palm Beach yachtsmen enjoyed shooting at the slow-flying birds as they approached their nests on the three-acre island. (Photo: Arthur Morris/Birds As Art)

Marjory Stoneman Douglas forever changed the way Americans view the Florida Everglades with her book *The Everglades: River of Grass*, which distilled the 6,000-square-mile marsh into its fierce and elemental beauty. "The clear burning light of the sun pours daylong into the sawgrass and is lost there, soaked up, never given back," she wrote. "Only the water flashes and glints. The grass yields nothing."

For much of this century, Douglas has been associated with the Everglades. In the 1920s she wrote editorials opposing its draining and urging its protection; in the 1930s and 1940s she served on a committee seeking to form a Florida national park, and she lobbied the federal and state governments for its creation. In 1947, the year she wrote *River of Grass*, she sat on the dais with President Harry S. Truman during the dedication of Everglades National Park. However, despite her previous efforts, Douglas once said that she did not become truly involved with the Everglades and the effort to save it until 1967, when, at the age of seventy-eight, she wrote *Florida: The Long Frontier* and became one of the country's leading environmental activists.

In 1969 Douglas founded Friends of the Everglades, now a 5,000-member group pledged to the protection and restoration of the South Florida wetland. She traveled all over the state speaking on behalf of the Everglades and railing against its enemies: foot-dragging politicians, land-hungry developers, the sugar industry, the U.S. Army Corps of Engineers. In 1994, at the age of 104, when she felt that the state was retreating from its commitment to restore the Everglades, and to the dismay of Florida legislators, she publicly demanded that her name be stricken from the Marjory Stoneman Douglas Everglades Forever Act of 1994.

Douglas, who died in May at the age of 108, found beauty in unexpected places. She once wrote of the turkey vulture, "I never knew how beauty grew; From ugliness, until you flew ... Teach me how to go; Like you, to slip such carrion ties; And lift and lift to high, clean skies, Where winds and sun and silence ride, Like you, oh buzzard, glorified." She also found a beauty worth defending in the Everglades, one of the least hospitable regions on earth.

—TED LEVIN

Dutcher, tried to buy the island from the federal government, but Roosevelt instead issued an executive order proclaiming the island "a preserve and breeding ground for native birds." Pelican Island thus became the first federal bird refuge.

Roosevelt would rapidly proclaim many more. Frank Bond, an Audubon director who became chief clerk in the Department of Agriculture's Land Office, wrote up the executive orders and letters of transmission for the president to sign for the next fifty-nine refuges, many of them sites originally proposed by Bond, Dutcher, and other Audubon leaders. Gradually, bigger refuges were added for game species: In 1905 Congress authorized Roosevelt to set aside part of the Wichita Forest in Oklahoma as a reserve for elk, and in 1908 Congress itself established a National Bison Range in Montana.

At first, these refuges were merely places where hunting would be prohibited. Because local constables didn't enforce laws on federal lands, and the Bureau of Biological Survey that watched over the refuges

had no funding to provide wardens, the government relied upon wardens paid by Audubon to patrol and enforce the bans on shooting, especially in the bird rookeries of the Atlantic Coast.

It soon became clear that just banning hunting in the refuges wasn't enough. In 1917, commercial interests seeking to irrigate more farmland persuaded the Bureau of Reclamation to divert the Klamath River from Lower Klamath Lake Refuge in Oregon. William Finley, Audubon's field representative, declared, "By the summer of 1921, this whole country had been changed into an alkali desert in places and other parts to a wide, dry peat bed which took fire and burned to a depth of several feet . . . The flocks of birds that formerly whitened the lake and tule marshes were gone."

The heart of the matter was this: If wildlife was to survive, we would have to protect and manage large quantities of suitable habitat.

Americans learned this lesson largely from their experience with waterfowl. It was clear by the 1920s that ducks and geese were being squeezed into smaller and smaller areas where, in denser winter concentrations, they became easier prey for hunters and animal predators. Waterfowl populations were declining, and it was apparent that loss of habitat was more devastating to them than shooting. Audubon president Gilbert Pearson explained, "With the more complete occupation of arable lands, agricultural interests have in recent years gone extensively into the project of draining swamps and marshlands. . .As a result the wildfowl feeding grounds in many regions have been destroyed." By 1924, an estimated 71 million acres of wetlands, an area twice the size of New England, had been drained. Declared Pearson, "Many voices are heard crying out that at least some places be preserved where migratory water-

Above: *Egrets nest in the low shrubbery on the Nature Conservancy's Virginia Coast Reserve, a 45,000-acre barrier island wilderness of sandy beaches, salt marsh, and upland that is accessible only by boat. The Conservancy has 1,340 preserves totaling more than 10 million acres in the United States, the world's largest private system of nature sanctuaries. (Photo: Stephen J. Krasemann/ The Nature Conservancy)*

Pages 96-97: *With its wings set, black flight feathers spread to brake the descent, and pink feet down like an airplane's landing gear, a snow goose swings into the landing pattern at Bosque del Apache National Wildlife Refuge in New Mexico. The snow goose population has exploded in recent years to the point where the birds are destroying their coastal Arctic nesting habitat by overgrazing. The U.S. Fish and Wildlife Service and Canadian Wildlife Service are looking for ways to drastically reduce their numbers, including longer goose hunting seasons. (Photo: Arthur Morris/Birds As Art)*

fowl may find food and shelter." While some states were acting to create refuges for big game and upland birds, most states felt that because the Migratory Bird Treaty Act had given the federal government control of waterfowl, they had no further responsibility to the resource. Those that accepted responsibility lacked funding to save wetlands on an adequate scale, leading Pearson to conclude, "To take up the task of purchasing and reserving such areas, we must look to the United States Government."

Hunters agreed. John Burnham of the American Game Protective Association (AGPA) noted that wealthy hunters could buy up good waterfowl hunting grounds, but others could not. He declared in 1919, "Public shooting grounds must be established for the rank and file of the gunners who cannot afford to belong to an expensive club." In that year, Tennessee established the Reelfoot Lake Public Shooting Grounds, across the Mississippi River from the Big Lake National Wildlife Refuge in Arkansas.

Burnham and others believed that because hunters would be the chief beneficiaries of waterfowl refuges, they should pay all the costs. George Lawyer, Chief U.S. Game Warden, had suggested that a federal waterfowl stamp, sold at post offices and affixed to state licenses, would provide funds with which to buy vanishing wetlands and manage them for waterfowl production. Burnham endorsed the idea. A bill introduced by Senator Henry New of Indiana and Congressman Dan Anthony of Kansas, entitled "The Public Shooting Grounds—Game Refuge Act," called for a land purchase program for refuges and public hunting areas funded by the sale of stamps. Many congressmen disliked the idea of a new tax, and many hunters opposed the plan because they feared that once wetland areas were in the hands of the government, they would be closed to hunters.

The most important opposition came from those who simply opposed hunting on the refuges. This conflict led to bitter words and even a lawsuit between Burnham and William Hornaday of the New York Zoological Park. Burnham had gone west at the

Sacramento National Wildlife Refuge lies in the Central Valley of California between the Coast Range and the Sierra Nevada, and the mountains funnel a million or more ducks and geese looking for a wintering place into its fields and ponds. Snow geese like these birds and look-alike Ross's geese are abundant, but a spotting scope will find rare Aleutian Canada geese and Tule white-fronted geese. The refuge also hosts half of the continent's pintail duck population and a wide variety of other waterfowl, wading birds, and shorebirds. (Photo: Daniel J. Cox/Natural Exposures)

age of seventeen to work as a hunter supplying a Wyoming ranch with meat. He wrote about his experiences and that led to a job from 1891 to 1896 as business manager for *Forest and Stream*. He learned conservation from Grinnell and when he settled in the Adirondacks, he exposed public officials who illegally hunted deer with dogs, and that led to appointments as Chief Game Protector for the State of New York and later Fish and Game Commissioner. The AGPA was formed in 1911 with seed money from arms and ammunition manufacturers who wished to safeguard sport hunting by promoting uniform game-protection laws and establishing refuges. Burnham was urged by Roosevelt, Grinnell, and nature writer John Burroughs to become its first president. He took the job and lobbied hard for the Migratory Bird Protection Act and later, the Migratory Bird Treaty; after that, he sat on the Biological Survey's advisory committee that helped form regulations under the Migratory Bird Treaty enabling act.

Hornaday had himself been an avid hunter, shooting enthusiastically to bag specimens for the National Museum, in Washington, D.C., where he was chief taxidermist. In 1895, he became director of the New York Zoological Park. Long active in trying to restore bison in the West, he became convinced that "the progressive extinction of all United States game and near-game is rapidly proceeding," and that "98 percent of it is due to merciless and determined shooting." Habitat loss was, in his mind, a "minor factor." Hornaday was given to intemperate rhetoric and to arguing the character of people rather than the more complicated biology of wild creatures. (He once confidently accused California hunters of exterminating bobwhite quail, despite the fact that the species had never existed in the state.) When duck populations plummeted in the 1920s he demanded shorter seasons and smaller bag limits. When the public shooting grounds bill came before Congress,

Hornaday vigorously opposed it because he felt the sole purpose of the new refuges would be to provide hunting opportunities, and that the refuges would simply be "slaughter pens" where waterfowl could be concentrated and "butchers" could easily kill them. Hornaday accused Burnham of duplicity. Burnham sued for libel, and compelled Hornaday to make a meek apology.

The conservation movement, which had been strongly unified during the campaign for the Migratory Bird Treaty Act of 1918, was deeply divided. Pearson urged Audubon members to support the refuge bill, but the fight split the National Association of Audubon Societies into warring factions. Some put up billboards calling hunters "murderers." Willard Van Name, the Yale biologist, wrote a pamphlet accusing Pearson of being simply an agent of the gun manufacturers. Pearson felt obliged to tell Audubon members, "It is to the organized sportsmen of America that we are chiefly indebted for the preservation of the game birds and animals which exist in the country today," and to remind them that hunting licenses paid the salaries of the officials who looked after both game and non-game species. He stressed that the bill would set aside as refuges lands that were currently hunted and protect them from future drainage. And he negotiated a compromise by which the bill stipulated that 60 percent of the lands set aside as refuges would be "inviolate sanctuaries" and only 40 percent open to hunting.

With conservationists divided, the refuge bill failed in three Congresses. Then, Senator Peter Norbeck of South Dakota, working closely with conservation groups, stripped away the federal licensing and public shooting grounds features of the bill, and renamed it The Migratory Bird Conservation Act, and it and a companion bill in the house carried by

***Pages 98-99:** The bulbous trunks of ancient bald cypress rise from the still water of Reelfoot National Wildlife Refuge in Tennessee. The refuge embraces part of the Reelfoot Lake basin, which was formed in 1811–12 by a series of cataclysmic earthquakes that caused part of the Mississippi River floodplain to fall thirty-five to forty feet. As many as 200 bald eagles winter at Reelfoot, flying out from their swamp-forest roosts to feast on the lake's wealth of fish. (Photo: David Muench)*

The male redhead is one of North America's most handsome ducks and an increasingly rare sight in many areas because its marshland nesting habitat has been drained. One of the diving ducks, the redhead feeds on submerged vegetation. The male's courtship call sounds a lot like a cat's meow. (Photo: Tim Fitzharris/Minden Pictures)

August H. Andresen of Minnesota simply called for refuges to be funded individually by Congressional appropriation. Audubon members wrote between 200,000 and 300,000 letters urging its passage. Burnham opposed the bill because he felt Congress would never authorize enough money on a refuge-by-refuge basis.

The Migratory Bird Conservation Act passed in 1929, but Burnham soon proved right in his predictions about funding. In 1929 the Depression made federal funding scarce. It was followed by the seven-year drought of the 1930s, that dried out the wetlands so necessary to waterfowl, especially in the nation's midsection. Ducks returned in the spring to parched potholes and blowing dust, and they failed to reproduce. At the end of 1929, the Biological Survey cut bag limits from twenty-five to fifteen birds. In 1930, Canadian wildlife officials reported the year's duck hatch was less than half that of the previous year's abnormally low levels. By 1934, winds sweeping over the arid plains would roll up sheets of topsoil and drop them as dust over Boston and Atlanta. Hornaday and others called for an end to all waterfowl hunting. Still, little of the $10 million authorized in the Migratory Bird Conservation Act for purchase of refuges was released by Congress.

Franklin D. Roosevelt, elected president in 1932, sought to dovetail a program to retire marginal farmlands with the demand for wildlife refuges, and thereby to provide, at one stroke, relief for impoverished farmers and funds for acquisition of waterfowl breeding and feeding grounds. In 1934 he appointed Jay "Ding" Darling, wildlife biologist Aldo Leopold, and Thomas Beck of More Game Birds (the forerunner of today's Ducks Unlimited) to serve as a special committee to devise such a program.

A convoy of juvenile American coots paddles past tall ranks of marsh grass lit by the evening sun at Utah's Fish Creek National Wildlife Refuge. A remote oasis at the edge of the Great Salt Desert that once was a Pony Express station, Fish Creek is fed by powerful springs that gush 70 degree water, attracting a wide variety of water birds including nine kinds of ducks, trumpeter swans, white-faced ibis, and black-necked stilts. (Photo: Daniel J. Cox/ Natural Exposures)

At the peak of his influence as a Pulitzer Prize–winning cartoonist, Jay Northwood "Ding" Darling was read by millions. Because of his commitment to publicizing the dangers of pollution and wildlife extinction, he was asked by President Franklin D. Roosevelt, in 1934, to head the U.S. Biological Survey—now the Fish and Wildlife Service. Darling's legacy includes a 5,030-acre wildlife refuge in Florida that bears his name, the National Wildlife Federation, and the Federal Duck Stamp Program, which uses fees charged to hunters of migratory waterfowl to acquire and protect habitat.

Newspaper cartoonist Ding Darling at work. A critic of President Franklin Roosevelt's conservation policies, he was co-opted to head the federal Biological Survey but remained a thorn in FDR's side. (Courtesy J. N. "Ding" Darling Foundation)

Darling would become one of the key conservation figures of the 1930s, and would later have a National Wildlife Refuge named for him. A newspaper reporter and political cartoonist, he had served as a Fish and Game Commissioner in Iowa where, with Aldo Leopold's help, he had developed a progressive twenty-five-year wildlife plan. Reflecting on the loss of wetlands, he often said, "Ducks can't nest on a picket fence." He insisted "that wildlife is properly entitled to its share of land and water, and to have such areas set aside solely for its use and benefit."

While Beck felt the crisis could be solved by breeding ducks in captivity and releasing them into the wild, Leopold felt that natural systems should be relied upon for a long-term solution. Darling sided with Leopold and wrote a report calling for a $25 million "national wildlife restoration program," including rapid and widescale purchase and restoration of wetlands. The new refuges would build water structures to reflood once productive marshes, and plant fields of grain to feed waterfowl. "Once set aside for wildlife," declared Darling, "these lands should never be released to other uses except upon clear proof that such use is of essential importance to the welfare of the Nation."

In 1934, Roosevelt, promising funding for such refuges, convinced Darling to become chief of the Biological Survey. When Darling took the job but got no funds, he went around the president, working with Senator Norbeck to get Congress to appropriate $6 million for land acquisition. That same year, Darling and the conservation community resurrected the Duck Stamp idea and got Congress to pass the Migratory Bird Hunting Stamp Act. Darling himself designed the first stamp.

When Roosevelt would not ask Congress to tax hunting weapons and ammunition to fund conservation work, Darling persuaded the arms and ammunition manufacturers to volunteer ten percent of their profits to waterfowl restoration, a feat that paved the way for

__Opposite, top:__ Embracing nearly 20 million acres of North America's wildest landscape, from the taiga lakes on the south slope of the craggy Brooks Range to the ice floes of the Beaufort Sea, the Arctic National Wildlife Refuge is one of the world's largest nature preserves. In the short Arctic summer, the coastal plain teems with birdlife. The tundra is splattered with ponds where swans nest while ptarmigan cackle in the willows, Lapland longspurs hide their nests among dwarf poppies, and (when lemmings are plentiful) snowy owls stand watch at every vantage point. (Photo: Art Wolfe)

__Opposite, bottom:__ Pristine salt marsh is one of the scarcest habitats on both the Atlantic and Pacific coasts, and the National Wildlife Refuge system includes several critical areas. For example, ACE Basin National Wildlife Refuge in South Carolina helps protect an undeveloped estuary where the Ashepoo, Combahee, and Edisto rivers come together. On the other side of the continent, San Francisco Bay National Wildlife Refuge has saved the last scraps of 300 square miles of marshland that existed in Gold Rush days. Two endangered species depend on the Bay refuge—the secretive California clapper rail, named for its clattering call in the mating season, and the fascinating salt marsh harvest mouse, which eats salty pickleweed (or glasswort) and drinks saltwater. No other mouse can make that claim. (Photo: Gilbert S. Grant/Photo Researchers)

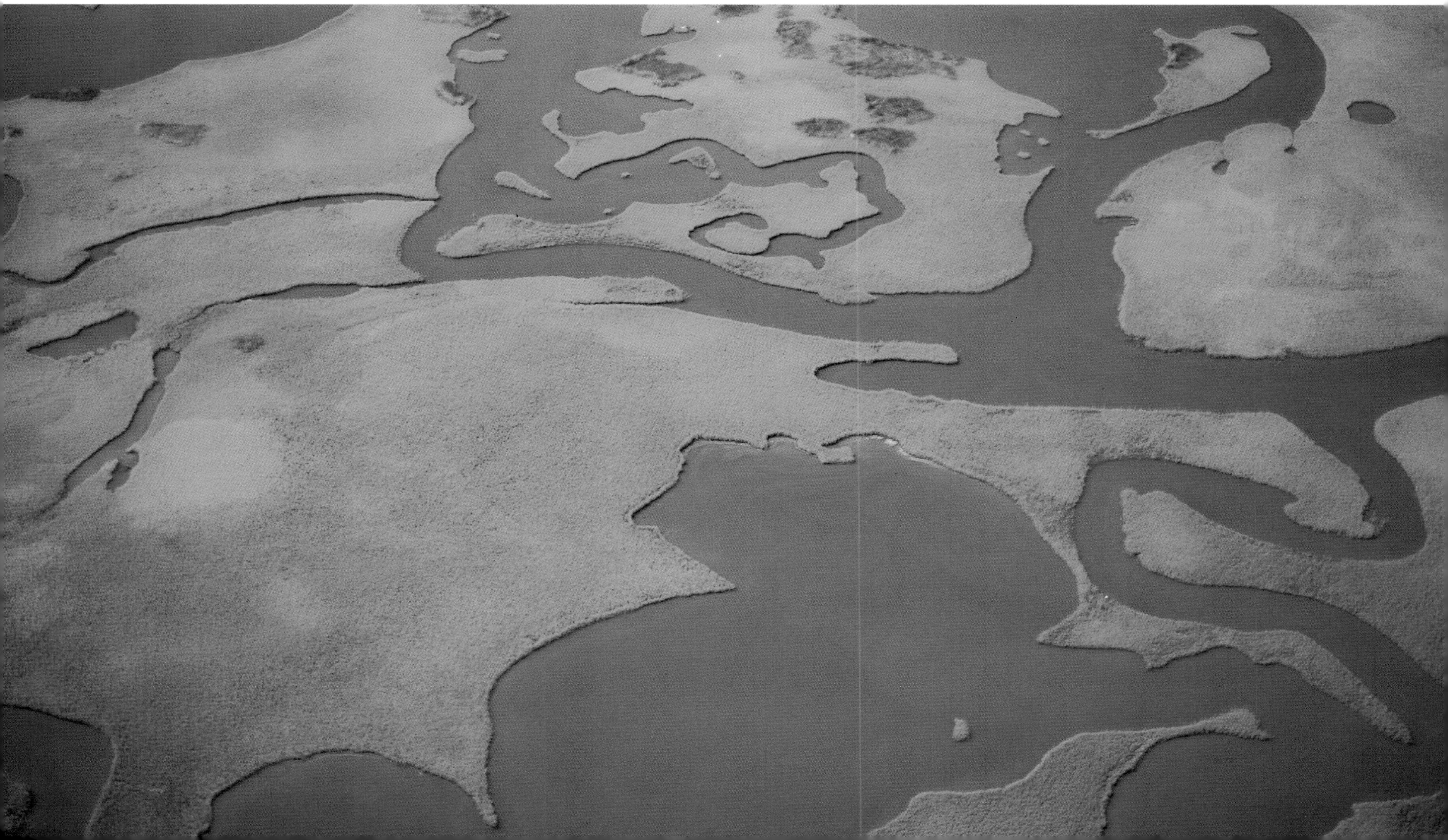

Ding Darling painted the first Migratory Bird Hunting Stamp—a pair of mallards—in 1934. The Duck Stamp's 50th anniversary was celebrated with William Morris's painting of a pair of wigeons. Funds raised by stamp sales to sportsmen and nonhunters alike have helped expand the National Wildlife Refuge System to more than 500 individual refuges totaling 92 million acres. (Courtesy U.S. Department of the Interior)

passage in 1937 of the Pittman-Robertson Act, which taxed sporting equipment and shared the proceeds with state wildlife agencies seeking to set aside refuge lands and improve their own management capacities. To bolster support for wildlife programs, Darling brought together hundreds of local, county, and state organizations concerned with wildlife conservation to found the National Wildlife Federation, and—leaving the Biological Survey in 1935—became its first president.

In the middle of 1933 there were only 1.6 million acres in the federal wildlife refuge system. By the end of the decade 100 new refuges had been established and the system had grown to 13.5 million acres. Duck Stamp funding guaranteed that most refuges would serve waterfowl production, but there would also be refuges for Florida panthers, Columbian white-tailed deer, desert bighorn sheep, and other featherless creatures.

By the end of the decade, Ira Gabrielson, Darling's successor at the Bureau of Biological Survey, could speak confidently of a national wildlife refuge system, with plans "to restore every acre of marsh ground in the breeding range of these birds that can possibly be restored," by purchase or by paying farmers to reflood marginal farmlands to make them fit for waterfowl. "We look forward to the time," declared Gabrielson, "when we will be able to say that the refuge areas in this country are adequate to insure, so far as human provision is possible, that not one remaining species of American wildlife will perish from the face of the earth."

Gabrielson's vision was overly confident. Thirty years later Congress would pass the Endangered Species Act to try to protect species the refuges had failed to protect. Fifty years later, wetlands were still disappearing. But by 1940 the nation had made a commitment to preserve wildlife by protecting habitat, and to provide funding sources for the effort. By 1998, there were more than 500 refuges covering more than 93 million acres.

Today, tiny Lake Merritt, in Oakland, California, is as much overshadowed by the vast federal refuge system as it is by high-rise offices and urban dissonance. The pump and filter for a 200,000-gallon freshwater pond inside a fenced-in "Duck Feeding Area" haven't worked for ten years. The city, preoccupied with crime and urban poverty, hasn't found the funds to fix them. Just across the fence from the pond is a row of benches. At one end sits a young man in a hooded sweatshirt with a radio blaring angry rap music; at the other end sits an old man in an open-collared shirt with a radio blaring "Shine On, Harvest Moon," in voices reminiscent of 1908.

Thus do opposite ends of the century contend for the soul of the nation's oldest public refuge.

***Opposite, top:** The steep seaside cliffs and grassy hills of Seal Island in the Gulf of Maine harbored a huge settlement of Atlantic puffins until they were exterminated by fishermen who landed at night, spread herring nets over the boulders, and caught the birds when they left their burrows at dawn. The last twenty-five or so pairs were taken in 1887. Used by the U.S. Navy as a bombing range during World War II, Seal Island is now a national wildlife refuge and one of the sites where the National Audubon Society is restoring puffins and other lost seabirds such as Arctic and common terns and razorbills. (Photo: Arthur Morris/Birds As Art)*

***Opposite, bottom:** A thousand or more desert bighorn sheep, a subspecies that was hunted almost to extinction, own the high cliffs of Kofa National Wildlife Refuge near Yuma, Arizona. President Franklin Roosevelt set aside Kofa from public domain lands in 1939, in large part due to letters from Boy Scouts alerted to the plight of the statuesque mountain rams. Waterholes that have been enhanced for the benefit of the bighorns also lure other desert creatures such as kit foxes, ringtails, and mule deer, and birds like the cactus wren and brown towhee scratch out a living in the washes and canyons. (Photo: Galen Rowell)*

1940

Big, Beautiful, and Doomed?

1940

Big, Beautiful, and Doomed?

by Frank Graham Jr.

BY THE 1940s at least three species of North America's largest, most spectacular birds were, by the accounts of knowledgeable naturalists, on the way to extinction. One thread that ran through and bound together the birds' dismal recent histories was the fact that nobody knew very much about them. The adjectives commonly used to describe one or all of these birds—"striking," "majestic," "noble," "splendid"—hadn't helped them in a nation no longer hostile, but largely indifferent to the plight of nonhuman creatures. In fact, the features that prompted the praise were words that had brought the birds to the notice of the kind of people who liked to shoot big animals. The ivory-billed woodpecker, California condor, and whooping crane seemed as dead as, well, the dodo.

"Today it is almost extinct," Arthur Cleveland Bent wrote in 1939 of the ivory-bill in his *Life Histories of North American Woodpeckers,* "and indeed during the past fifty years long periods have elapsed when no individuals have been reported from any part of their range."

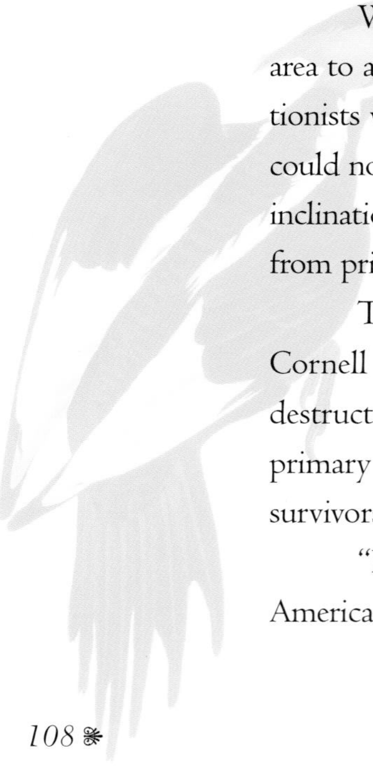

Where did the remnant members of these species spend most of their time, and when did they move from one area to another? What were their breeding and feeding habits? How could they best be protected? One of the conservationists who asked these questions was John Baker, president of the National Audubon Society. Baker knew the questions could not be answered without concentrated field studies, but neither the universities nor government agencies showed any inclination to fund the research. In 1937 he drew up an Audubon Research Fellowship Plan, then found financial support from private donors and contracted with two universities to carry out long-term studies on the ivory-bill and the condor.

The highest priority was the ivory-bill, the largest woodpecker in the United States. Several ornithologists from Cornell had recently located a few of them in the virgin cypress and bottomland forests of the Deep South. The destruction of those old forests, as lumbermen cut their way through even the most remote areas, was certainly the primary reason for the ivory-bill's decline. Compounding the loss of its habitat was an intensified hunt for the few survivors in an era when collecting the skins and eggs of rare species was still a popular pastime.

"Right here I might offer a word of advice to the ivory-billed woodpecker, now the rarest bird on the North American continent and one that is going to come in for more and more attention," the humorist Will Cuppy wrote in

Pages 106-107: *The month of March on the Platte River between Grand Island and Kearny, Nebraska, means sandhill cranes. Bound for Canadian nesting grounds, the sandhills make a leisurely stop to forage in stubble fields during the day and roost in the safety of mid-river sandbars at night. That's where these birds are heading as the sun sets on the Platte, and they will have a lot of company. The sandhill is the most abundant of the world's fifteen crane species with a population estimated at half a million birds, compared with the somewhat larger whooping crane whose wild population approaches 200. The rusty-gray sandhills have been enlisted in various schemes to help the big white whoopers. (Photo: Thomas D. Mangelsen)*

Page 109: *The whooping crane may be the most famous bird on the world list of endangered wildlife. Never a common bird like the sandhill crane, the whooper's principal breeding range in the mid-1800s followed a broad arc of prairie from central Illinois to Alberta, Canada, and there may have been 700 nesting pairs before settlers arrived with their plows and guns. The historic low point in the whooping crane chronicle was 1942, when only sixteen birds returned to their wintering grounds at Aransas National Wildlife Refuge on the Texas coast. (Photo: Arthur Morris/ Birds As Art)*

Left: *The only images of the ivory-billed woodpecker are paintings like John James Audubon's dramatic interpretation (left) and rare black-and-white photographs taken in Louisiana in the 1930s by the great Cornell University ornithologist, Arthur A. Allen. (Courtesy Library of Congress; NAS/Photo Researchers).*

1941. "Keep away from birdlovers, fellows, or you'll be standing on a little wooden pedestal with a label containing your full name in Latin: *Campephilus principalis.* People will be filing past admiring your glossy blue-black feathers, your white stripes and patches, your nasal plumes in front of lores, your bright red crest, and your beady yellow eyes. You'll be in the limelight, but you won't know it. I don't want to alarm you, fellows, but there are only about twenty of you alive as I write these lines, and there are more than two hundred of you in American museums and in collections owned by ivory-billed woodpecker enthusiasts. Get it?"

Cuppy's comments were all too apt. At about the same time, an Audubon official, Richard Pough, encountered a well-known New England taxidermist and his son who had just returned with more than two hundred birds, many of them rare, that he had shot in Florida. As there were still sightings of ivory-bills and even dubious rumors about the long-extinct Carolina parakeet in the state's backwoods, Pough questioned the taxidermist. "He said no, he was quite sure the parakeet was extinct," Pough reported, "but that they spent a lot of time hunting for ivory-bills, [which] always turned out to be the pileated woodpecker. There is no doubt in my mind that they would have shot any ivory-bills they might have found."

Audubon gave James Tanner, a Cornell graduate, a research fellowship to study the woodpecker. Tanner and his colleagues slogged through Louisiana swamps, listening for the peculiar toy trumpet-like calls of the ivory-bill and the occasional rapid-fire succession of "kents" that it uttered as it flew through the forest. When he caught glimpses of the birds, he dutifully noted the long-horned beetles and other woodboring

What probably were the last ivory-billed woodpeckers in America haunted virgin cypress and hardwood forests in Louisiana, where the birds handily peeled away the tough bark of lofty trees to expose wood-boring insects. There have been unsubstantiated reports of ivory-bill sightings in the decades since lumbermen ravaged the giant woodpeckers' last-known habitat, but most conservationists believe the species is extinct. (Photo: Yva Momatiuk and John Eastcott/ Photo Researchers)

insects they fed on as they peeled the bark from big trees or chiseled with their stout bills into the limbs and trunks. Tanner trailed a young ivory-bill for more than three months after it had left the nest in a tree cavity, studying the sequence of early plumage stages as the bird matured. And, in the process, he described the historical shrinkage of the species' range as the old forests went down.

The results of Tanner's study became the first of the Audubon Research Reports, which were to set a standard for later ornithological monographs on individual species. John Baker had hoped that it would supply the detail needed to establish a conservation plan to rescue the ivory-bill. But instead of a prescription for recovery, the report turned out to be the obituary of a species now embalmed in extinction.

Greater hopes were held for a study that Audubon supported partially through the University of California at Berkeley. The researcher selected for a thorough survey of the condor's plight was Carl Koford, a zoologist and forester in his early twenties, characterized by his supervisor as "a person equipped with the perseverance, ruggedness, and natural instincts for observation which the field study of the California condor absolutely required."

The condor is one of the most majestic of birds, gliding on a nearly ten-foot wingspan over southern and central California's ridges and chaparral-covered slopes. Beginning in 1939, Koford backpacked into the mountains, scaled cliffs, and kept watch at nests, sometimes living in a cave "not unlike that occupied by the condors a half-mile away." He pursued all available clues to the species' dwindling numbers and, after a break for military service during World War II,

An eight-day-old California condor chick was photographed by Audubon researcher, Carl Koford, in a cave nest part way down from the top of a sheer sandstone cliff. Condors raise but one chick, and the fledgling period is five months. For another two months the young condor depends on its parents for food. (Photo: NAS/Photo Researchers)

__Opposite:__ The shooting of rare birds for museums and private collections played a significant role in the loss or near extinction of many species. For example, there are more than 300 taxidermy mounts, skins, and skeletons of whooping cranes in museums around the world. Carl Koford said he knew of 130 California condor mounts and skins in museums, more than twice the number in the wild when he was undertaking his arduous study of the species for the National Audubon Society in the 1940s. The huge, bare-headed bird (seen here) also was a tempting target for hunters. Others died from feeding on sheep carcasses that had been laced with poison to kill bears, cougars, and coyotes. (Photo: Tom McHugh/Photo Researchers)

picked up his vigils again in 1946, when he estimated the total condor population at about sixty individuals. At that level, the loss of one or two birds a year could put this huge vulture beyond recall.

Koford knew that its biological pace, in which individuals matured and reproduced slowly, already put the species at a disadvantage. He found that a condor "requires at least five years to reach sexual maturity," while it produces "perhaps three young, and some of these young die before becoming mature." He also identified the chief human threats to the bird, among them wanton shooting, collecting for "scientific purposes" (one collector he knew of assisted at the shooting of ten condors for museum specimens during the 1920s), habitat destruction, and poisoned carcasses set out by ranchers to control predators and other "pests."

But Koford, a passionate and committed conservationist, considered the prime threat to the condor's recovery to be public apathy. People can be persuaded to embrace the protection of an eagle, a puffin, or an egret, but a vulture is not likely to inspire the same enthusiasm.

"You'd be surprised at the number of people who ask me how I can admire a bird that 'eats dead things,'" a condor defender remarked in later years. "Well, I always look straight at a person like that and I ask, 'Tell me, sir—do you eat live things?'"

Koford's recommendations for strong federal condor-protection legislation (more likely to be heeded than state or local laws), specifically the closure of large areas of rugged mountain lands critical to the species' survival and widespread education campaigns, were in the main disregarded. It was almost inevitable

California condors prefer trees to rocks for perching and roosting, conifers over hardwoods, and dead trees over living ones. (Photo: Carl Koford/NAS/Photo Researchers)

then that the rest of the condor story would become less than gratifying. The following decades revealed even more insidious hazards, including DDT contamination over vast areas of condor habitat, leading to a decline in the birds' ability to produce young. There were also fatal cases of lead poisoning caused by condors eating the bullet-riddled carcasses of mule deer, coyotes, and other mammals shot by hunters or predator-control agents.

By the late 1970s, Audubon officials were urging the U.S. Fish and Wildlife Service to take more aggressive action to save the species. Biologists on the scene estimated that the population of California condors had dropped to about thirty-five birds, which had the effect of making federal bureaucrats reluctant to squander money on what they now considered a hopeless case. But eventually the agency replied to Audubon, saying in effect, "Put your money where your mouth is!" The Society responded (grudgingly, perhaps, because of suspicions among some of its senior officials that the government's defeatism was on target) by contributing $300,000 to jump-start the program and lobbying Congress to fund the Fish and Wildlife Service's involvement.

Field studies in 1980 showed the situation to be even worse than anyone had believed: Barely more than twenty condors existed. Emergency measures, including a captive propagation program and the tracking of birds through radio telemetry (the latter requiring the trapping of condors in nets at baited sites and the fitting of these wild birds with tiny radios) became extremely controversial in California. Several environmental groups, Audubon chapters among them, protested this "hands-on" approach. Some of the protesters seemed to be saying that this noble bird ought to be allowed to lapse gracefully into extinction.

"The condor is not an electric toy to play with, rough up, manipulate, blindfold, manhandle, peer into, wire for sound, tinker with the great wings of, double-clutch, or put on crutches or behind bars," insisted the Sierra Club's David Brower, the "arch-druid" of the conservation movement. "The wilderness

"The beauty of a California condor is in the magnificence of its soaring flight," Carl Koford wrote in the conclusion of his report to the National Audubon Society. "A condor in a cage is uninspiring, pitiful and ugly to one who has seen them soaring over the mountains." Others in the conservation community shared his view and it led to a major rift over whether the last wild condors should be trapped for a captive breeding program, a step that proved to be the correct one. (Photo: Jesse Grantham/ National Audubon Society)

within the condor and the wilderness essential to it have rights. We deplore the over-curiosity of biologists who would invade that privacy."

But federal and Audubon biologists on the Condor Recovery Team countered that the species was dying off in isolation. "The literature published by some opponents of the Fish and Wildlife Service's Recovery Program gives the impression that the bird is a lost cause and [that they] are counting on its extinction to teach us all a lesson," said Assistant Secretary of the Interior Nathaniel P. Reed. "According to this idea Americans would be so ashamed at the bird's demise that they would wholeheartedly support future efforts to set aside sufficient habitat for wide-ranging creatures."

Hopes rose for a while that the condor was holding its own. Five mated pairs supplied the observers with valuable information about their diets and movements through the species' range. But a serious split had appeared in the recovery team. The Fish and Wildlife Service resisted Audubon's attempts to "politic" against the subdivision and development of land holdings within the condor range, while at the same time it wanted to take more wild birds into captivity. Audubon biologists backed away, hoping to keep more of these birds in the wild to see how they dealt with changing conditions, including environmental hazards.

Then, in the mid-1980s, disaster struck. Five or six condors, at least one from each of the remaining active pairs, simply disappeared. The Fish and Wildlife Service, perhaps weary of the whole collapsing venture, acted unilaterally in deciding to capture all the remaining wild condors and put them into the captive breeding programs at zoos in San Diego

The gray whale—a primitive, coastal species not closely related to other cetaceans—is extirpated from the Atlantic, gravely endangered in the western Pacific, and flourishing in the eastern Pacific. This last population has been protected since the 1930s by regulations promulgated by the League of Nations. This—combined with the protection of breeding and nursery lagoons by Mexican authorities—has been enough to bring the California gray whale back from the brink of extinction. Despite other whale species not recovering, the grays are now close to their pre-whaling population of 20,000 to 23,000. In June 1994, the California gray whale became the first and only marine mammal to be taken off the endangered species list. —TED WILLIAMS

Gray whales in the eastern Pacific use protected lagoons on the Mexican coast as nurseries. (Flip Nicklin/Minden Pictures)

and Los Angeles. Audubon's court challenge to that decision failed. Biologists trapped the remaining condors, and the species, after soaring for millions of years over the rugged mountains of the Southwest, had been eliminated from the wild.

Out of the squabbling, indecision, and finger-pointing has emerged a born-again condor. The breeding program increased the total from a low of twenty-one or twenty-two individuals in 1982 to about 150 in 1998. Releases of captive birds into the wild has had a success rate of better than fifty percent, excellent by any standards, so that the thirty-five free-living condors exceed the highest number since the 1970s. Despite bungling within and outside Audubon, the program saved the condor from certain extinction, but the long-term outcome remains unclear. As the writer, Kenneth Brower, remarked, "When the vultures watching your civilization begin dropping dead from their snags, it is time to pause and wonder."

The object of the third and most heart-warming of the great avian recovery efforts, begun in the shadow of World War II, was the whooping crane. In a sense, this campaign would have been voted most likely not to succeed because, until the mid-1950s, no one even knew where the primary group of cranes nested. A few nonbreeders from the population summered throughout southern Canada. But the breeding pairs of these spectacular long-legged birds—at five feet North America's tallest species—simply vanished for 170 days a year!

Any account of the whooping crane's return from near-oblivion must focus on the work of a

***Opposite, top:** Unlike songbirds and shorebirds, cranes and other large water birds are not programmed at hatching to migrate long distances using celestial and magnetic cues. They learn by traveling with adults. But if crane chicks are hand raised in the wild, there will be no experienced birds to show them the way. Experiments with sandhill cranes and ultralight aircraft have proved that young birds will accept the pilot and plane as a surrogate parent, though there are risks in flying a fragile craft in the company of birds with seven-foot wingspans. (Photo: Arthur Morris/Birds As Art)*

***Opposite, bottom:** A lone white bird in a crowd of sandhill cranes at Bosque del Apache National Wildlife Refuge in New Mexico is one of the last survivors of a disappointing attempt to create a new flock of whooping cranes in the Rocky Mountains. Over a fourteen-year period, workers collected nearly 300 whooper eggs and placed them in sandhill crane nests at Grays Lake National Wildlife Refuge in Idaho. As researchers expected, the young whoopers followed their foster parents to the Bosque and returned with them to Idaho in the spring. The flaw in the plan was the refusal of the whoopers to mate with their own kind. They were sexually imprinted on the sandhills. (Photo: Gary R. Zahm)*

***Pages 118-119:** Robert Porter Allen virtually invented the science of conservation ornithology with his classic study of the roseate spoonbill in Texas and Florida for the National Audubon Society. Spoonbills usually weren't hunted for the millinery trade because their pink feathers quickly fade. However, the slaughter of egrets for their breeding plumes caused spoonbills, which shared the colony sites, to desert their nests. By 1920 only two dozen breeding pairs of spoonbills survived on the entire Gulf Coast, where once there were thousands. (Photo: Arthur Morris/Birds As Art)*

***Page 119:** Bob Allen had seen his first whooping crane while working with roseate spoonbills on the Texas coast, not guessing that a full-scale study of the birds would be his first assignment for Audubon after World War II. (Photo: NAS/Photo Researchers)*

remarkable field biologist, Robert Porter Allen. Allen led Audubon's research department, giving it a vision and an eminence that shone like a beacon during this critical era in wildlife conservation. By the time he joined Audubon's staff in the early 1930s, most of the primary legislative battles had been won. The plume birds enjoyed protection from the millinery gunners, song birds prospered under the Migratory Bird Treaty Act, and game bird populations recovered from earlier lows as the nation's hunters accepted reasonable bag limits. Yet, as we have seen, several of the large "glamour" species failed to adapt to landscapes dominated by humans.

Bob Allen was a romantic naturalist. As a boy in rural Pennsylvania, he had drenched himself in the prose of popular writers on natural history. Birds were his passion. He corresponded with ornithologists and used his first paycheck from the National Guard to treat himself to a pair of binoculars. He grew into a stocky, dark-haired young man, gentle and humorous, the best of companions in the field or after hours. An outdoorsman to the core, he fretted under organized scholarship, limiting his higher education to brief sojourns at a couple of colleges. Adventurous young men in the 1920s often chose between the life of a hobo or that of a sailor. Allen opted for the sea and, after cruising the world on tramp steamers for three years and surviving a shipwreck in the Philippines, landed in New York.

Determined to find a job that coincided with his love for birds, Allen joined the Audubon staff and soon, on Maine's offshore islands where early wardens had protected various gulls and terns, he surveyed the first known nesting colonies of the great black-backed gull in the United States. Shortly after the studies of the ivory-bill and the condor got underway, Audubon assigned him to check on another avian case, the roseate spoonbill. The monograph he produced on this pink, long-legged wading bird of the Gulf Coast is a

fascinating life history of a fascinating bird, given added weight by suggestions for its conservation. Allen, living at times like a spoonbill among sand flies, burrowing crabs, and an occasional crocodile, spent three years shadowing the birds on Florida and Texas shores until World War II sent him back to sea. (The spoonbill has recovered nicely in the intervening years.)

Allen returned from naval duty to encounter his greatest challenge. The whooping crane was thought to be another lost cause. Any glimmers of hope were generally sparked by false information—reports of an upswing in the species' population when observers mistook a distant band of big white birds, such as white pelicans or snow geese, for whoopers. In 1940 the American Ornithologists' Union estimated that "chances for the survival of the whooping crane are probably only slightly better" than for the ivory-billed woodpecker.

And that was before the species hit absolute bottom in the winter of 1941–1942. Only twenty-one of the birds were counted that season, fifteen of them in the Aransas National Wildlife Refuge on the Texas coast and another six in the Louisiana marshes. The establishment of the refuge in 1937 was perhaps the step that saved the species. The Louisiana group dwindled one by one over the next few years, picked off by hurricanes or perhaps poachers, and the lone survivor was taken into captivity.

Curiously, the two groups of whooping cranes were not in contact. The Louisiana birds had developed a sedentary lifestyle, permanent residents of the marshes. Earlier in the century, a few of the Texas whoopers had bred in Saskatchewan, but no nests were found there after 1922. From then on, the remnant group flew farther north every spring, exposing itself to hunters, storms, and all the other hazards of migration. The whereabouts of the Texas cranes' breeding grounds remained one of the century's most puzzling ornithological mysteries.

Allen, on assignment from a joint Audubon-Fish and Wildlife Service research contract, began studying the whoopers after they returned to Aransas from their terra incognita in the fall of 1946. "Some years before," Allen recalled, "when on the Texas coast working with roseate spoonbills, I'd seen my first whooping cranes and wondered what poor unsuspecting soul would some day be assigned the rugged task of making a full-scale study of them. I hadn't the slightest notion it would be me."

Now he had in his sights the entire world population of whooping cranes (aside from a woebegone captive pair), their numbers only slightly increased by then to twenty-five birds. Despite the protection afforded by the refuge, hazards abounded. Oilmen had drilled wells near the refuge islands, and coastal Texas's new Intracoastal Waterway ran for ten miles through the cranes' prime habitat. Most disturbing of all was a bombing and machine-gun target range the Air Force had laid out on Matagorda Island nearby; only protests by the Canadian government, based on its Migratory Bird Treaty with the United States, closed down the lethal activity.

Allen learned that it wasn't easy to observe these shy birds. But after watching them consort with cattle in the marshes, he fashioned a huge, portable observation blind in the shape of a bull, stretching a "skin" of heavy red canvas over a light framework of wire and painting on such details as eyes, a nose, and assorted wrinkles. It was, as Allen admitted later, "a bum steer." He had to abandon the scheme after a live bull challenged this awkward intruder in the marsh.

Yet in one way or another Allen managed to collect data on the cranes' preferences in food and habitat. He counted individual food items as well as he could through binoculars and supplemented those observations by analyzing the birds' droppings—and even by sketching their great tracks in the soft mud of feeding ponds.

"Here and there would be a broken carapace and two hard legs, disconnected and lying in the mud and shallow water just as they had fallen when broken off," he wrote. "Here the great birds had fed on blue crabs, digging them out of their burrows, grabbing them as they sought to escape by running off in their skittish, sidewise manner. The whole story, from beginning to end, lay before us in a characteristic diagram."

But the frantic part of the work came when the birds began leaving Aransas in spring. Like geese, the parents and young stay together for a year or so, but in small family groups rather than in large flocks. This fragmentation of the world's only band of whooping cranes made them difficult to follow. Searches in earlier years by American and Canadian biologists had not been successful in following the birds to their breeding grounds.

Allen's strategy was to track them by means of reports called in by observers along the route as the cranes flew north to Canada through Oklahoma, Kansas, Nebraska, and the Dakotas. One of Allen's

most important duties at this time was to make sure the birds received intense publicity on their flight so that hunters in spring or fall would not confuse them with other species and shoot them. And as a result of the publicity, all of America seemed to follow the birds' progress with rapt attention.

Year after year Allen tracked the cranes northward but always lost them over the vast deserted muskegs and lakes beyond Alberta and Saskatchewan. His flights and those of waterfowl biologists from the two countries proved fruitless until 1954. In July of that year, he received an electrifying call. A firefighting crew en route by helicopter to a remote area in the Northwest Territories had spotted a family of whooping cranes on the ground in Wood Buffalo National Park—a park set aside by Canada in 1922 as a refuge for bison!

Overflights by the Canadian Wildlife Service confirmed the sighting. But even helicopters equipped with floats could not land in that watery, forested area and it was too late that summer to mount an overland expedition. The next summer Allen and several Canadian colleagues finally received the call that the cranes were back in their breeding territories. The biologists, after an exhausting and frustrating thirty-one-day search by helicopter, canoe, and endless bush-whacking, eventually reached the site. Their reward was a glimpse, through the thickets, of two whooping cranes. It wasn't until they flew over the area a month later that they saw the pair's two offspring and other successful nesting pairs in the vicinity.

"It was a trying experience to slog about over that rare country and not be able to keep the whoopers in sight," Allen wrote later. "But by then we were thoroughly conditioned to trying experiences. Nevertheless, we had a feeling of being hopelessly earthbound. Even the fairly numerous black bears and moose, seen later from the air, kept out of our sight. As was the case with the whoopers on the ground, we saw only their tracks. In spite of this drawback, we kept busy and we learned much. We were on the spot, we gazed at its features and we felt of it with our hands. Most important of all, it is no longer unknown. It is no longer terra incognita."

What is the whoopers' terra incognita, their

The breeding grounds of the Aransas Refuge whooping cranes in the muskeg wilderness of Canada's Wood Buffalo National Park remained hidden until 1954 despite a tireless search by Audubon Society researcher Bob Allen, who traveled 20,000 miles by small plane and another 6,000 miles by Jeep in the vain hope of spotting the towering birds on their nests. (Photo: Thomas D. Mangelsen)

***Pages 120-121:** Whooping cranes hunt for their favorite food, blue crabs, in the Aransas tidal marsh. While there have been heartening increases in whooper numbers in recent years, biologists say the species remains at considerable risk. The wintering area lies along the Gulf Intracoastal Waterway, a crowded shipping lane for petroleum and chemicals, and an accidental spill could devastate the habitat and kill a large percentage of the 180 extant whoopers. (Photo: Tom Bean)*

Shangri-la? As Allen discovered, it is a pothole region of some 500 to 600 square miles in the northern part of the park, lying twenty-four miles south of Great Slave Lake and hemmed in by rivers clogged with fallen trees. It is a watery world, a checkerboard pattern of shallow ponds and lakes, separated by narrow ridges that support dense thickets of dwarf birch, willows, and black spruce. The whoopers have little to fear from predators in their wet fortress, though fires are a hazard. Allen and his colleagues, listening to their shortwave radio from their little camp on a ridge that rose like an island from the surrounding muck, heard descriptions of severe thunderstorms that had touched off raging fires on similar ridges.

"A short distance upstream, in a meager growth of poplars, there was a deserted beaver dam and the series of little waterfalls made a pleasant and somewhat drowsy music," Allen wrote. "Accompanied by the wind in the spruce tops, this plaintive sound was constantly in our ears. Other songs were contributed by the birds that kept close to the river thickets—chiefly song sparrows, Lincoln's sparrows, and redwings—while snipe winnowed in the twilight that passes for night in that latitude, and bitterns boomed from marshy ponds off to the east. Now and then we heard the guttural notes of sandhill cranes from the same direction, and on a few occasions, the clear trumpet calls of whooping cranes usually from off to the west where a wandering pair or family group may have been trespassing on the territory of our neighboring nesting pair."

Those trumpet calls still sound. In the years since then, under strict protection all along the lengthy migration route from Aransas to Wood Buffalo National Park, the little group has grown steadily into a genuine flock, numbering more than 180 whoopers by 1998. Biologists, using birds taken from "surplus" eggs in Canada, have also created a nonmigratory flock in Florida. Extinction is no longer an imminent threat for the species, a development that would have profoundly gratified Bob Allen (he died in 1964), who had approached his study of the great bird with compassion and respect.

"For the Whooping Crane there is no freedom but that of unbounded wilderness, no life except its own," Allen wrote during those uncertain days in the 1950s. "Without meekness, without a sign of humility, it has refused to accept our idea of what the World should be like. If we succeed in preserving the wild remnant that still survives, it will be no credit to us; the glory will rest on this bird whose stubborn vigor has kept it alive in the face of increasing and seemingly hopeless odds."

***Right, top:** The song of the red-winged blackbird—a pleasant, gurgling konk-la ree—accompanies a display of fire-engine red epaulets. (Photo: Jim Brandenburg/Minden Pictures)*

***Right, bottom:** Another familiar sound in marshes across the northern states and Canada is the eerie whistling effect that common snipe produce by vibrating their tail feathers during zigzag display flights. (Photo: Darrell Gulin)*

1950

The Dawn of Ecology

1950

The Dawn of Ecology

by Jon R. Luoma

THE YEAR IS 1959: a summer camp on the shores of a crystalline lake in northern Michigan. In the amber light of a summer evening, a gaggle of boys and girls runs and skips like the children of Hamlin, following not a piper but a pickup truck. The truck is winding a serpentine path between the cabins, the small chapel, the clapboard nature center, and the log main lodge. From a machine mounted on the back of the truck spews a rolling, blue-white fog, and the children zig and zag out of that sudden, magical cloud, laughing and shouting, until one adult has the good sense to tell them to stop.

Still, the fogging on that evening in 1959 continues, for it seems good, and right, for any modern summer camp to spray its mosquitoes and gnats into oblivion every few days. Why, after all, should children have to put up with the annoyance of insect bites when the wonders of the modern age could simply make pests vanish in a cloud?

The active ingredient in the fog spewing from that truck was a chemical called dichlorodiphenyltrichloroethane, more notoriously known in later days as DDT. By then DDT was one of the cheapest and most readily available of a panoply of new insecticides. It was the age, as a popular television commercial liked to put it, of "better living through chemistry." Pesticides in general had been declared safe, and products such as DDT seemed to be a modern wonder on the level of antibiotics. Indeed, Swiss chemist, Paul Muller, who had discovered in the 1930s that DDT could effectively kill insects, had later won a Nobel Prize for Medicine for his work.

For the American military during World War II, the compound indeed proved to be a superb preventative for scourges ranging from mosquito-borne malaria to disease-carrying lice. DDT was deadly for insects but, unlike previous insect-poisons, not (or so it seemed) toxic in any way to the people exposed to it. By the 1950s, DDT's use—and the use of such chemically similar organochlorine insecticides like endrin and dieldrin—had gone far beyond the control of disease carriers. Farmers virtually poured DDT and its chemical cousins on their fields, and foresters on their woods. Down at local hardware stores, suburban homeowners stocked up on pesticides in hopes of staging mosquito-free barbecues. Cities routinely doused elm trees at street-side in an attempt to control Dutch elm disease (caused by a fungus carried by a bark beetle). Even the National Park Service sprayed trees in Yosemite National Park to exterminate naturally occurring defoliators such as leaf miners—not actually to save trees that had evolved to defend themselves perfectly well against any lasting harm from these insects, but simply to improve the trees' appearance. In the modern American home, aerosol cans loaded with bug poisons had become as ubiquitous as fly swatters, and dousing the house with insecticide

An American robin tends to its nestlings. Because of their feeding habits, robins in particular suffered from the spraying of village and urban trees in a futile attempt to stop the spread of Dutch elm disease. Uncountable numbers of the birds died in agonized tremors after eating DDT-laden earthworms that in turn had munched contaminated leaf litter. The story of the robin and the elm, based on events on the Michigan State University campus, became the centerpiece of Rachel Carson's landmark book Silent Spring. *(Photo: John Shaw)*

an attempt to control Dutch elm disease had eradicated entire waves of migrating robins and other birds. Wallace and fellow scientist Richard F. Bernard would later report that of sixty-nine dead robins picked up on the campus, ninety percent harbored loads of DDT in their brains (well above proven lethal levels)—chemicals accumulated from the DDT contaminated worms they had eaten. Fully forty other species of birds appeared to be at risk from the pesticide.

There was other disturbing news from southern Louisiana. In 1958 came the first of what would be a cascade of reports of fish and wildlife mass deaths in the lower Mississippi River and tributary streams. By 1959, the state's Water Pollution Control Division noted that it was receiving reports of fish floating belly-up on streams "on an almost daily basis," but only after a massive kill of fish, including 150-pound gar and 70-pound catfish, along with crabs, wading birds, and otters, would wildlife officials trace the problem to contamination of sediments containing the pesticide endrin.

Although the wholesale spraying of organochlorine pesticides continued unabated, the issue had captured the interest of another biologist, Rachel Carson, who also happened to be a lucid, forceful writer. Her previous books, including *The Sea Around Us* and *The Edge of the Sea*, were popular tributes to ocean ecosystems—tributes written in graceful

A reserved, private person, Rachel Carson became the center of the most intense firestorm in the history of conservation with her book *Silent Spring*. She had taught zoology at the University of Maryland from 1931 through 1936. As a marine biologist and editor of publications for the U.S. Bureau of Fisheries, she had acquired the professional background that gradually led her to fame. Her books about the oceans, notably *The Sea Around Us*, which won the National Book Award for nonfiction in 1951, had established her as a best-selling author of international repute.

These experiences gave Carson a unique preparation for her role as environmental catalyst. During the 1950s she began to hear disquieting reports from scientific colleagues about widespread declines among bird and mammal populations. She started to look more deeply into the working of ecosystems and the effects of new, long-lasting agricultural chemicals such as DDT. In 1962, after four years of exhaustive research, she published *Silent Spring*.

A campaign organized and funded by the food and chemical industries blanketed the press. Critics, almost all of them with close ties to growers and the marketers of chemicals, called Carson a "cultist" and her book a "hoax." Many of the attacks were sexist. "I thought she was a spinster," one critic remarked. "What's she so worried about genetics for?"

But as a presidential commission was to show, Carson was a careful scientist who did not urge the rejection of all pesticides but, rather, a ban on those shown to be most harmful, and the judicious use of the others. Using the research of prominent biologists, she had built a convincing case that biological systems were being upset by the careless use of pesticides.

Carson's work survived the carping of other scientists, and her book prompted federal agencies to ban DDT and to control other contaminants some years before they would otherwise have acted. It took one woman, with the skill to penetrate to the roots of biological reality and an eloquence that made her findings heard, to touch off the Age of Ecology.

—Frank Graham Jr.

and impassioned prose. Carson, who had worked for many years at a U.S. Fish and Wildlife Service research center, would have preferred to continue writing about marine ecosystems, but she had become alarmed about the ecological effects of DDT and related pesticides.

A careful researcher, Carson began her pesticide studies in the late 1950s, and labored for four years to produce the book that was to become something more than an alarm about pesticides, but virtually the touchstone of the modern environmental movement. "For many years, environmentalism was a disjointed, inchoate impulse; a revolution waiting for a manifesto," former *New York Times* environmental reporter Phillip Shabecoff would write more than thirty years later. That manifesto, he added, "came in a remarkable book by a remarkable woman."

A remarkable book indeed. *Silent Spring* appeared first in serialized form in the spring of 1962 in *The New Yorker*; portions also were excerpted in *Audubon*.

Carson's story could have been insufferably dry and technical, but her approach was both lyrical and emotionally powerful. For instance, she began the book with a sort of reverie turned grim, in an imaginary "town in the heart of America," a lovely burg surrounded by farms and woods and lush fields,

Right: During World War II, DDT was credited with stopping a lice-borne typhus epidemic among GIs in Italy—along with other miracles—and by 1945 it was being billed as a cure-all for the world's insect woes. But National Audubon Society officer, Richard Pough, saw the future when he told a writer for The New Yorker that the widespread use of DDT would devastate all kinds of wildlife, including "most of the birds we have now." Pough's warning went unheeded. (Photo: Alfred Eisenstaedt/Nature Conservancy)

Far right: Rachel Carson in her favorite element—the sea. The rancorous, decade-long fight to ban DDT that followed the publication of Silent Spring in 1962 was the coming-of-age of the environmental movement. (Photo: Shirley A. Briggs)

streams filled with trout and host to "countless birds." But suddenly, like a place out of science fiction, her town and surrounding countryside are visited by a "strange blight," an inexplicable environmental illness, in which birdsong falls silent, where children and adults become sick, and where the only clue is a mysterious white powder that has "fallen like snow upon the roofs and the lawns, the fields and streams."

The East Lansing experience offered Carson and her readers a poignant lesson from the real world. "Few birds were seen in their normal foraging activities," she wrote of the Michigan robins just after elm trees were sprayed the first time, in 1955. "Few nests were built; few young appeared. The pattern was repeated with monotonous regularity in succeeding springs. The sprayed area had become a lethal trap in which each wave of migrating robins would be eliminated in about a week. Then new arrivals would come in, only to add to the numbers of doomed birds seen on the campus in the agonized tremors that precede death."

Carson also noted that freezers at the Cranbrook Institute of Science in Bloomfield Hills, Michigan, were filled with the carcasses of sixty-three species of birds, collected after a public appeal for birds that might have been killed by spraying.

Carson was especially successful in conveying a pair of related points little understood by the general public. The first was that DDT and its related pesticides were effective for the precise reason they constituted such a threat to the environment: they were extraordinarily persistent. Because DDT breaks down at a predictable rate, scientists had been able to document that toxic residues of DDT from spraying programs in the 1940s still remained in the environment more than

Opposite: *A peregrine falcon dismembers a city pigeon. Thirty years ago, this noble bird of prey seemed doomed because few young falcons were being raised to replace an atrophying adult population. In 1975, an intense search of 557 historic peregrine breeding sites in the forty-eight contiguous states and southern Canada turned up just sixty-two breeding pairs. Only eight of 100 known aeries in California were in use, and no peregrine had been seen on a cliff east of the Great Plains since 1970, when a lonely male in Vermont scanned the skies in vain for a mate. (Photo: Arthur Morris/Birds As Art)*

Right: *A council of bald eagles on a snag along the Alaska coast. While the Alaskan eagle population remained strong, the bird was only recently removed from the endangered species list south of the Canadian border. Like the peregrine, osprey, and other birds at the top of the food chain, bald eagles that ate contaminated prey laid thin-shelled eggs that were crushed during incubation. Scientists eventually determined that DDE, the metabolite of DDT, blocks normal calcium accumulation during eggshell formation. (Photo: Thomas D. Mangelsen)*

Pages 134-135: *A bald eagle snags a salmon in its powerful talons. During fall spawning runs on Alaskan rivers, hundreds of birds collect from points as far away as California to feast on dead and spent fish. (Photo: Thomas D. Mangelsen)*

a decade later. Bound to the fatty tissues of living things, these compounds did not dissolve in water, and thus were almost impossible to flush from cells. And she explained the astonishing and troubling fact that these persistent compounds tend to accumulate over months and years, their toxicity actually magnifying by hundreds or thousands of times in organisms such as ospreys, peregrine falcons, eagles, and other top-of-the-food-chain predators.

By 1960, National Audubon Society research director Sandy Sprunt IV would launch the Continental Bald Eagle Project, aimed at collecting data to determine if (as spotty reports were indicating) the national bird really was in a steep population decline. The project served as the linchpin for research on bald eagles and other birds of prey across the U.S., collecting and distributing field research reports, and bringing researchers together to compare notes. Sprunt later observed, "This project was instrumental in showing that DDT had a large part to play in the pollution of the environment and the decline of several raptor species, including the bald eagle."

In *Silent Spring*, Carson succeeded in conveying a message perhaps even more vital than the one about pesticides alone: her best-seller brought knowledge about the interconnectedness of nature to a new and broad audience, introducing these concerned readers to the basics of the previously obscure science called ecology, which examines connections and relationships in nature. Carson introduced a non-scientific audience to the ecologist's notion that plants and animals in nature are profoundly interdependent.

The immediate response to *Silent Spring* from the pesticide industry was ridicule—of both the book and its author. Carson, pronounced one chemical industry spokesman, was merely "a fanatic defender of the cult of the balance of nature." Her book, another said, was a "hoax."

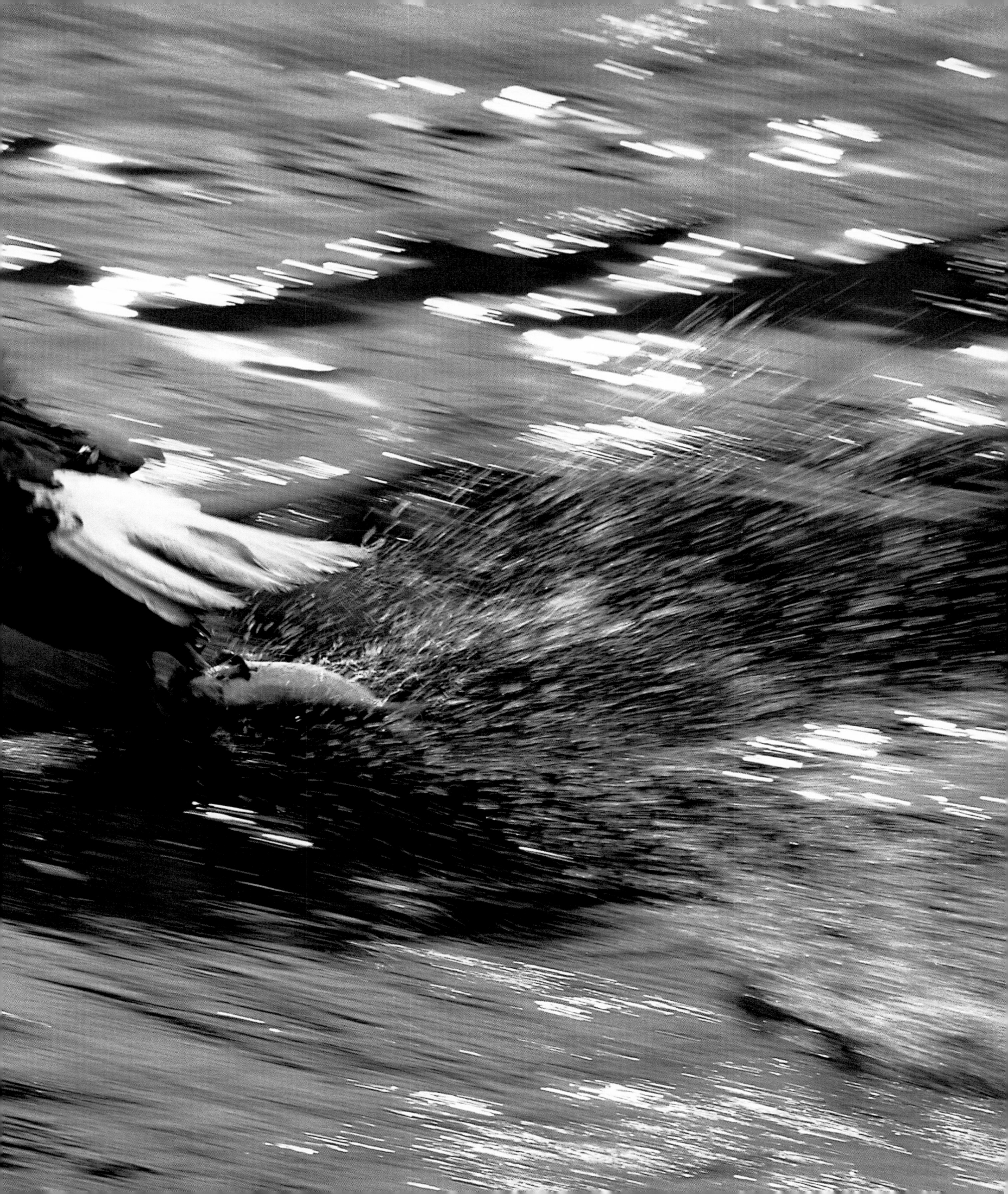

Business Week suggested *Silent Spring* focused on "the unproved possibility" that DDT and related pesticides could cause environmental and even human harm. Even the magazine *Sports Illustrated* (which would in later decades carry forceful articles about the dangers of toxic chemicals, acid rain, and global warming) took up the industry cause, insisting that "wildlife populations all over the nation are bigger and healthier than ever, not in spite of pesticides, but in many cases because of them." The article concluded that the very "prosperity of wildlife today is a direct result of man's—particularly American man's—increased ability to control his own environment."

At least one critic was bluntly, and wrongly, dismissive. Carson's book was a flash in the pan, declared a chemical industry trade magazine. The industry should "take heart from the fact that the main impact of the book will occur in the late fall and early winter—seasons when consumers are not normally active buyers of insecticides."

To the contrary, Carson's work galvanized environmental concern across the country, nowhere more dramatically than at the National Audubon Society, which soon became as closely identified with the DDT fight as Carson herself. In fact, a look at a periodical index for the decade shows a remarkable pattern: although there was a burst of publicity about Carson and the pesticide issue in the months directly following *Silent Spring*'s publication, the issue soon virtually disappeared from the pages of America's magazines, except for one: *Audubon*. Reflecting the continuing concern of staff naturalists and scientists, National Audubon Society president Carl Buchheister and vice president Charles Callison seldom missed a chance in their regular columns during the early 1960s to call attention to the latest scientific finding, environmental debacle, or political move having to do with DDT or related insecticides. By late in the decade, the magazine was carrying detailed feature articles about the scientific and public policy aspects of the DDT story.

In 1964, Buchheister was faced with reporting tragic news: Rachael Carson had died after a long battle with cancer. In that same column he pointed to astonishing reports of just how correct she had been, including the recent Louisiana fish and wildlife endrin disaster. "Who now can say that Rachel Carson was an alarmist?" he wrote.

In the wake of *Silent Spring*, a special commission appointed by President John F. Kennedy recommended in 1963 that persistent pesticides be used only in the most extreme cases: when urgently needed to control insects that were human disease carriers. The recommendation was ignored, and DDT overuse continued. But a determined, energized cadre of scientists and activists continued to examine the issue, eventually accumulating a veritable flood of evidence about how DDT affected eagles and other birds of prey. Laboratory studies showed that as DDT molecules built up in a raptor's body over time, the compound finally could be potent enough to induce the liver to generate enzymes that interfered with calcium metabolism, a process critical for egg-shell formation. Field studies of such widely distributed species as the peregrine falcon documented a worldwide collapse of populations that appeared to be linked to reproductive problems, including females laying eggs too thin-

Opposite: *A male American kestrel emerges from its nesting cavity in an ancient oak tree after feeding its four or five chicks. This pretty little raptor is as much at home in cities and towns as it is in open country, when it is usually seen perched on telephone lines or hovering over a field. Kestrels feed mainly on grasshoppers, mice, and small birds, especially house sparrows in urban habitats. (Photo: Daniel J. Cox/Natural Exposures)*

Peregrine falcon eggs hatch at a California breeding facility. In an historic and heroic rescue effort led by the Peregrine Fund, more than 6,200 captive-produced peregrine chicks were released at nest sites across the continent and tended mostly by volunteers until they took wing. By 1994, at least 875 pairs of peregrines occupied territories south of the Canadian forest, including 150 pairs in California and 159 pairs in the eastern and mid-western states. Like the bald eagle, the peregrine has been removed from the federal endangered species list. (Photo: Galen Rowell/Mountain Light)

shelled to survive until chicks hatched. Other studies of egg-shell samples from museums showed that although shell thickness had been stable before World War II, shells became notably thinner starting in the postwar years—just as DDT began to find widespread use. And more lab studies—like those on kestrels (close but non-endangered relatives of peregrine falcons)—proved that doses of DDT and a similar pesticide (dieldrin) administered in only mere parts per million could cause dramatic shell thinning.

The final death knell for DDT (and, eventually, many of its related pesticides) began when Victor

Far left: *A male osprey will devour the head and entrails of this ladyfish before it delivers the catch to his mate and their offspring. The North American osprey population also has rebounded since the use of DDT and other organochlorine pesticides was banned in the 1970s. (Photo: Arthur Morris/Birds As Art)*

Left: *Robins weren't the only songbirds victimized by DDT poisoning. Even small insect-eating migrants like the Canada warbler were in jeopardy. After a public appeal for birds that might have been killed by spraying, the freezers at the Cranbrook Institute of Science in Michigan were filled with the carcasses of sixty-three species. (Photo: Art Wolfe)*

Yannacone, an outspoken young Long Island, New York, attorney, successfully sued in 1966 to prevent DDT spraying on Long Island. The next year, Yannacone convinced a group of eminent scientists to join him in forming a brand-new environmental organization called the Environmental Defense Fund (EDF), aimed at using sound science to win the day in the courts. ("Sue the bastards!" became Yannacone's operative battle cry.) In its early months, the long-established and notably more conservative National Audubon Society provided the brash new organization with partial funding and a fiscal home—even handling its start-up funds until the EDF could meet Internal Revenue Service guidelines as a bona fide non profit organization. By the 1990s, EDF would become one of the largest and most powerful of the mainstream national environmental groups.

Under the EDF umbrella, Yannacone and his scientist-allies later successfully shut down DDT spraying for Dutch elm disease in Michigan, and again attacked DDT use for mosquito control in an exhaustive, six-month series of hearings in the neighboring dairy state of Wisconsin. The stage had been set: Although Congress could never bring itself to buck industry lobbyists and ban the pesticide, it would by 1970 create the U.S. Environmental Protection Agency (EPA), giving the new agency sweeping powers aimed at improving air and water quality and environmental health. And in 1972, amid a rising swell of evidence that the compound also posed a cancer risk to people, EPA administrator William Ruckleshaus effectively banned, by administrative order, DDT use for agriculture. By the next year, the EPA had virtually banned DDT for all uses. In subsequent years, many other organochlorine pesticides were outlawed as well. (However, although DDT has also been banned in most of the industrialized world, it continues to be used heavily across much of the developing world.)

Even as the DDT story was playing out its end game, the American public was becoming increasingly aware that a more widespread ecological sickness lay on the land and in the water. As remarkable as it might seem today, as the 1950s dawned there were virtually no effective federal laws or regulations prohibiting even some of the most ghastly kinds of water pollution—including raw industrial and municipal sewage that poured into rivers or lakes shared by more than one state. So effective had industry lobbies been against federal laws that even the first attempt at regulation, the Water Pollution Control Act which passed in 1948, had no teeth: it allowed for not even one full-time federal enforcement officer and included no provision to take offending companies to court.

As the 1950s proceeded, public disgust at what was happening to the nation's waterways grew increasingly intense until, in 1956, over opposition from industry, a newer, tougher (albeit weak by today's standards) federal Water Pollution Control Act passed Congress. Industry lobbyists had cajoled Congress into mandating that federal officials hold a "conference" with violators, rather than take formal legal action as soon as severe violations were discovered. Truly tough enforcement would have to wait for the founding of the EPA, more than a decade later. But in public relations terms this industry plan backfired.

With the new law backing them up, officials from the U.S. Public Health Service decided to focus first on water pollution in the Missouri River. A series of public conferences that began in 1957 propelled into public consciousness the troubling reality of how industry was treating American waters. The meetings revealed to the nation that in cities like Omaha, St. Joseph, and Kansas City horrendous pollution came from cattle slaughterhouses, turning a mighty river into a mighty sewer: tons of paunch manure (partially digested hay and grain) from millions of slaughtered cattle poured into the river, along with hair, lungs, and even hooves, as well as sewage from millions of homes and offices. The river,

Polluted water colored by dye from a textile mill pours into the Blackstone River in Massachusetts in the mid-1960s. At the time there were no effective federal laws prohibiting even the worst kinds of water pollution. (Photo: John E. Swedberg/Bruce Coleman)

said some in the region, had become "too thick to drink, too thin to plow."

Meanwhile, in the Northeast, the consequences of water pollution were becoming equally apparent. A 1958 study of Arthur Kill, the saline waterway that flows between New Jersey and Staten Island (a borough of New York City), found a 6.4-mile deoxygenated, utterly polluted slug of water "moving to and fro with the ebb and flood of the tide . . . apparently trapped there like a monster in some hideous primeval fen," commented writer Frank Graham Jr.

Nowhere was the water pollution problem to become more apparent, even to the point of absurdity, than in Lake Erie, the smallest of the Great Lakes, and in the Cuyahoga River, one of that lake's profoundly polluted tributary rivers. In many ways, Lake Erie's legacy was the legacy of the industrialization of America. The first European explorers had found Erie pristine. But by the mid-1800s, the population in the region had begun to boom, in large part thanks to the arrival of the Erie Canal and then the railroads. Settlers, seeking land and timber, streamed to the shores of the lake and its rivers and, as the Industrial Age came to the American heartland, the population boom continued. In just over 100 years Cleveland exploded from a tiny village into the fifth largest city in the United States, with 900,000 residents. Similar stories of explosive population growth played out on the lake's east end in Buffalo, on its west in Toledo, and northward in Detroit. By the middle of the twentieth century, the Lake Erie basin had become one of the world's great industrial centers, with much of its activity based around building and fueling the automobile.

Fire on the Cuyahoga: In June 1969, sparks from a railcar carrying molten slag ignited a slick of oil and solvents on Cleveland's open industrial sewer, which emptied into and was partly responsible for the near-death of Lake Erie. Televised images of a river on fire shocked the nation into demanding government action to stop the pollution of lakes and streams and led to passage of the Clean Water Act three years later. (Photo: Cleveland Press)

Should you find yourself someday sipping something trendy outside one of the popular waterfront night spots in a certain midwestern city, you might never guess that the gently flowing stream beside you was once the world's most infamous river. "Roll on, flaming river," satirist Randy Newman sang about the waterway that slices through Cleveland, a waterway once so polluted that it caught fire in 1969.

"That fire was a marvelous thing. It was a spark that ignited attention across the country," says Edith Chase, an Ohio chemist, housewife, and one of the many grassroots activists who waged a campaign back then to clean up the Cuyahoga River.

More than a century ago, an observer had complained that the river was befouled with everything from human sewage to animal carcasses, "with all manner of impurities floating on top." By the 1960s a quarter-million tons of oil and grease were spilling from the Cuyahoga's mouth and into Lake Erie. "This river used to be almost black and bubble like a cauldron," says Wayne Bratton, a charterboat captain.

The final absurdity came on June 22, 1969. Sparks from molten steel in a railcar showered the river, and the water—clogged with garbage and slicked with oil—raged into flames.

Today, much of the lower Cuyahoga remains an industrial river, winding through Cleveland toward Lake Erie past rows of factories and mills. But near the river's mouth, on the edge of downtown, cafés, nightclubs, and trendy shops line a river transformed. Thanks to local activists and to the Clean Water Act, passed by Congress in 1972, the Cuyahoga, even in downtown Cleveland, no longer smells anything like an open sewer. Wayne Bratton, with only a trace of irony in his voice, now calls it "the Scenic Cuyahoga." And the Cuyahoga Valley National Recreation Area, which was established in 1974 along twenty-two miles of the river and in the surrounding hills and forests, has become a popular destination for residents of Cleveland, a dozen miles downstream.

But like so many industrial rivers, the Cuyahoga is only clean in some ways. The sewage and grease and other visible offal that once clogged it are gone. But persistent toxic chemicals buried in river-bottom sediments continue to contaminate parts of the river. The federal government has plans to remove the pollutants, but it will take decades for the river to become truly clean once again. **—Jon R. Luoma**

But simultaneously, Lake Erie had begun to choke on the residue of industrial prosperity. By the late 1950s, some 18,000 tons of sewage, industrial chemicals and pesticides, and sediment were pouring into the lake every day. And the effects on the living ecosystem finally had become all too apparent in the life histories, or death histories, of the organisms that once had thrived in and around that aquatic ecosystem. For instance, the larvae of a large species of mayfly called *Hexagenia* can only survive in clean, oxygen-rich waters. Stanley Walkowicz, who today operates a wildlife museum for tourists on western Lake Erie's South Bass Island, remembers days before the 1950s when the big insects would hatch in such clouds they would bury the ground-mounted floodlights at a monument on the island. "They'd shovel them up. Sometimes they had to take a front-end loader to haul them away."

But sometime during the decade, the big mayflies had simply stopped hatching. Biologists were no longer able to find their larvae at the lake's bottom, finding

Page 142: *One sign of the gross pollution of Lake Erie by the 1950s was the disappearance of huge hatches of mayflies. (Photo: Gary Braasch)*

Pages 142-143: *A pristine freshwater marsh in the Midwest symbolizes progress made since the dawn of ecology in the 1950s. (Photo: David Muench)*

instead an abundance of worms that can tolerate filthy waters. Meanwhile, the catch of the lake's most prized game fish, the walleye, had plunged from 15.5 million pounds to only 3 million, and health officials had closed the lake's swimming beaches, so polluted were the waters with industrial and human wastes.

By 1966, vast expanses of Erie were choked with green algae, and its waters had lost so much oxygen to the tiny micro-organisms that thrived on the rich nutrients from sewage and other wastes that the journal *Science News* declared it "the dying lake." Once pure and blue, Erie, larger than eight of the states, had become an international symbol of the destruction of nature.

There was an air of hopelessness to all the pronouncements. Restoring the lake (and by implication other polluted lakes and rivers, and polluted air and land) would cost untold billions of dollars, *Science News* reported, and could take decades to achieve. Ecologist Barry Commoner's assessment was, if anything, even more gloomy: "It is entirely likely, I believe, that practically speaking Lake Erie will never be returned to anything approximating the condition it was in, say, twenty-five to fifty years ago."

And then in 1969 came the event that was so utterly grim, and at the same time so absurd, that it may have finally shocked a complacent nation into demanding determined action to clean up the environment: On June 22, a foul tributary of Lake Erie, the filth-clogged and oil-and-solvent-slicked Cuyahoga River, burst into flames when a bit of molten slag from a passing steel car landed upon it.

The environmental future may indeed have looked gloomy at the end of the 1950s, yet throughout the decade there had been signs of a steady turnaround in attitudes, not only among the public in general, but in Washington D.C. The 1960s would bring the beginnings of dramatic change. After furious lobbying from conservation groups led by The Wilderness Society, Congress would pass the Wilderness Act in 1964, and the National Wild and Scenic Rivers Act in 1968. And by the late months of that decade, simmering public discontent would generate support for tough new environmental legislation even among advisors to newly elected President Richard Nixon, a conservative who had shown little support for environmental issues in the past.

Paradoxically, the pesticide crises helped introduce the core concepts of ecology to a previously ignorant public. Until Rachel Carson's *Silent Spring*, ecologists had labored largely in obscurity. Notions that nature could be painlessly manipulated through clever technological tricks had been widespread: that rivers should be straightened, wetlands drained, predators wiped out to make life easier for game animals, and landscapes sprayed with chemicals to eliminate "pests." But Carson's best-seller, and the broad ecological messages that followed, would reach a new audience with a powerful story about the interdependent web of nature, and ultimately, the shared future of nature and humanity. With a message even more critical than any warning about pesticides, Rachael Carson had touched something new and deep in an audience larger than the core of already devoted conservationists. As Carson suggested, harm to a species in nature sets up a chain of consequences "like ripples when a pebble is dropped in a still pond."

1960

Before Earth Day

1960

Before Earth Day

by John G. Mitchell

IN THE MINDS OF MOST AMERICANS old enough to remember, the 1960s were a time of political turmoil and rapid cultural change. A war on poverty soon gave way to a war in Vietnam. Dissent stalked the groves of academe. Blood and ashes sullied the inner city. Indeed, there were so many memorable distractions in that raucous decade, it's easy for those of us who would enjoy and protect America's natural places to forget that the 1960s may well have framed the best years of our lives.

Now, a generation and a half later, the circumstances that made that period so rewarding for landsavers and other lovers of the out-of-doors are not often cited in the remembrance of things past. Some children of Earth Day still believe that the environmental movement was founded on April 22, 1970. Perhaps it would better suit those aging youngsters to know that without the movers and shakers of the early 1960s—and what they managed to accomplish through the rest of that decade—the earthy celebration might never have occurred.

So let us consider the fortuitous circumstances. There was, for openers, President John F. Kennedy's 1961 appointment of Stewart Udall as Secretary of the Interior. An Arizonan, Udall was a true conservationist, and there hadn't been one in that office since the resignation of Harold Ickes fifteen years earlier. Also in 1961, the Outdoor Recreation Resources Review Commission, authorized by Congress in the Eisenhower years, completed its exhaustive report under the leadership of Laurance S. Rockefeller. The commission proposed two principal recommendations. First, that the federal government should spend more money to acquire new parklands and, second, that some of those areas should be situated not in the boondocks but convenient to the nation's recreation-starved cities. Later, after the presidency passed to Lyndon B. Johnson, both Udall and Rockefeller could count on Johnson's wife, Lady Bird, to keep enhancement of scenic and recreational resources high on the chief executive's agenda.

Furthermore, the Congresses in session through the Kennedy-Johnson period, unlike those in later years, were inclined to lean favorably toward passage of laws and spending programs friendly to the environment. Not that there wasn't a good bit of sparring along the way: the Wilderness Act of 1964 had to be rewritten sixty-six times before the House and Senate could send it up for President Johnson's signature! Ultimately, the two legislative bodies passed a plethora of landsaving measures in that decade, thanks in part to the visionary leadership of men such as Gaylord Nelson of Wisconsin and John Saylor of Pennsylvania. And thanks also to the growing influence and communication skills of the Sierra Club and the National Audubon Society, the point players of a newly aggressive conservation

constituency no longer content to be dismissed as daisy sniffers and little old ladies in tennis shoes.

Sierra and Audubon both experienced rapid growth in membership during the sixties, largely as a result of the organizations' respective publishing efforts. The Sierra Club's best effort was its Exhibit Format Series, a line of handsome illustrated books conceived by Executive Director David Brower. For Audubon, the 1960s witnessed the transformation of *Audubon* magazine by editor Les Line from a house organ and birdwatcher's publication into an award-winning bimonthly that *The New York Times* would call "The most beautiful magazine in the world." But *Audubon* wasn't just a pretty read. Among its regular contributors was Charles Callison, a tough but soft-spoken Missourian (and Audubon Society executive vice president), whose reporting on national conservation issues often helped shape the policies of the day.

And what a feast of good things the confluence of these circumstances served the nation. In addition to effecting the Wilderness Act, the 1960s ushered in the greatest expansion the National Park Service had yet experienced in its ninety-year history. This included the inception of the first nationalized lakeshores and riverways to be preserved as pristine wilderness areas, a national trails system, and a program to designate wild and scenic rivers across America.

Moreover, in fulfilling one of the recommendations of the Outdoor Recreation Resources Review Commission, Congress in 1964 established the Land and Water Conservation Fund, a trust whose funding was cobbled together from offshore oil leasing revenues and other government receipts in order to purchase new federal parks and refuges and provide matching grants to the states in order to create state parks.

Clearly the Wilderness Act was among the greatest of all 1960s victories. It was, essentially, an American idea, however far removed from the thinking of mainstream Americans. After all, mainstream Americans and their Colonial predecessors had struggled for 200 years to subdue and tame the wilderness, to make the dark of the forest light enough, to silence the howl of the wolf. Yet even in the nineteenth century certain poets and philosophers could be heard actually praising the wild country, with one—Henry David Thoreau—going so far as to declare wildness to be "the preservation of the

Pages 144-145: *An evening thunderstorm is followed by a dramatic rainbow over Yaki Point in Grand Canyon National Park. One of the memorable battles of the 1960s pitted conservationists against the federal Bureau of Reclamation. Having drowned the rainbow-hued wonderland of Glen Canyon on the Colorado River under Lake Powell, the dam-builders planned their next reservoir in the Grand Canyon itself. (Photo: Tom Bean)*

Page 147: *The ferny Lady Bird Johnson Grove of ancient trees in Redwood National Park is a special place honoring the First Lady who helped keep the preservation of America's scenic resources high on her husband's agenda. (Photo: Carr Clifton/ Minden Pictures)*

Above: *Among the visionary leaders of the conservation movement in the turbulent 1960s were (left to right) Congressman John Saylor of Pennsylvania, Sierra Club executive director David Brower, and Senator Gaylord Nelson from Wisconsin. (Photo: Corbis/Bettmann/UPI; Karen Preuss/The Image Works; Corbis-Bettmann/UPI)*

A cold dawn at Trapper Lake in Colorado's White Mountain National Forest, with the high country of the Flat Tops Wilderness in the distance. An act creating a National Wilderness Preservation System became law with a stroke of President Lyndon Johnson's pen in 1964. (Photo: David Muench)

***Pages 150-151:** In Montana's Bob Marshall Wilderness, a formidable formation known as the Chinese Wall looms over a meadow decorated with the conical flower clusters of bear grass. Marshall was a forester who helped launch a new organization called The Wilderness Society in 1935. (Photo: Carr Clifton/Minden Pictures)*

world." Before that century was finished, New York State drew a protective line around its Adirondack Forest Preserve, and a constitutional convention would proclaim those lands "forever wild."

By most accounts, the genesis of a federal wilderness system was conceived by a young landscape architect and a forester working in the Southwest shortly after the end of World War I. This architect—Arthur Carhart—was responsible for designing a road into Trapper Lake, in the White Mountain National Forest of Colorado, so that the U.S. Forest Service might lease out the lakeshore for vacation cabin sites. The forester was Aldo Leopold, and his job was to assess the potential for logging in New Mexico's Gila National Forest.

As it turned out, both men had something altogether different in mind. Carhart, favoring scenery over cabin sites, managed to convince his superiors that a roaded development would destroy the value of Trapper Lake. Leopold—whose interesting forester-turned-conservationist life is discussed in the 1920s chapter—looked into the Gila and perceived a place devoid of roads, a place "big enough to absorb a two-weeks' pack trip." He talked his skeptical bosses into setting aside one half million acres of the Gila as a special primitive area, off-limits for loggers. By

1930, the Forest Service was busy bestowing "primitive" designations on other roadless areas throughout the West (although not all of them would escape the bulldozer and the ax).

It would take another forester, Robert Marshall, to inject some institutional grit into the business of defending these roadless areas. In 1935, Marshall rounded up Leopold, Benton MacKaye (an Appalachian Trail advocate), and Robert Sterling Yard (a former National Park Service publicist) to launch a new organization called the Wilderness Society. Over the next three decades this fledgling organization would dedicate its best effort—a "sacred charge," Yard had called it—to encourage policies and regulations to hold the spoilers of wilderness at bay.

Long after Marshall and Leopold and the other founding fathers had passed from the scene, Howard Zahniser, a journalist with roots in the wild Adirondacks, took over as executive director of the Wilderness Society and started drafting legislation to give the blank spaces on Uncle Sam's map the kind of permanent protection that safeguarded New York's forest preserves. Senator Hubert H. Humphrey, of Minnesota, introduced Zahniser's first version of a Wilderness Bill in 1957. The U.S. Forest Service and the National Park Service opposed it. Both agencies were too busy building roads into wild country. But by and by—or rather, by virtue of seven years and sixty-five more drafts of the measure—an act creating the National Wilderness Preservation System was signed in 1964 by President Lyndon B. Johnson.

The act established some fifty wilderness areas in national forests in more than a dozen states, including the million-acre Bob Marshall in Montana and the two-million-acre Frank Church-River of No Return in Idaho. Statutory wilderness, the law declared, would henceforth be recognized as an area "where the earth and its community of life are untrammeled by man, where man himself is a visitor

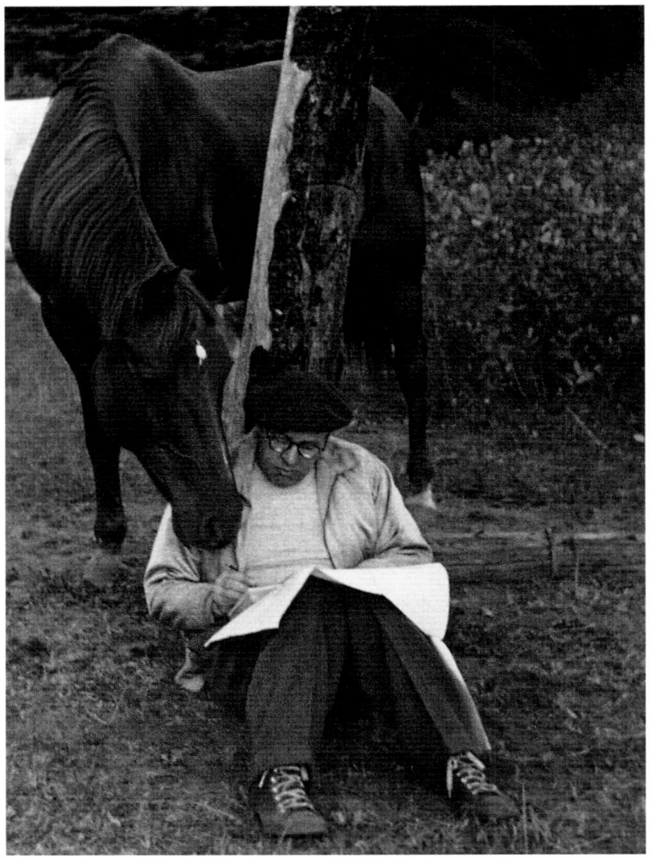

Left: *Howard Zahniser, a journalist who would lead The Wilderness Society, drafted the first Wilderness Bill in 1957. It was opposed by both the National Park Service and U.S. Forest Service since both agencies were busy building roads into wild country for their constituents—tourists who rarely left their cars, and the timber industry. (Photo: James Marshall/ The Wilderness Society)*

who does not remain." Moreover, the act stipulated that wilderness was to remain forever free of roads and other man-made structures.

That was just for starters. In the years since the measure was enacted, the Wilderness System has expanded beyond the national forests of the West to embrace roadless areas in the East, in national parks, wildlife refuges, and the public domain of the Bureau of Land Management. The Alaska National Interest Lands Conservation Act of 1980 more than doubled the system's size, with the addition of such sprawling wildlands as Gates of the Arctic and the icy ramparts of the Wrangell-St. Elias Range.

Today, that radical nineteenth-century idea that came of age in the 1960s is reflected in more than 600 separate wilderness units totalling 104 million acres. And although Wilderness U.S.A. now constitutes a patrimony larger than California, most forever-wilders would like to double even that. Who knows? With any kind of luck in the coming century, they just might get a fair piece of it.

If the National Park Service exhibited some disdain for statutory wilderness in the early 1960s, and by most accounts it did, the sour mood likely reflected a schizophrenia that had been built into that bureaucracy when it was established in 1916. Congress had directed the agency "to conserve the scenery and the natural and historic objects and the wildlife" within the lands assigned to it. So why, some top guns at the agency reasoned, was it necessary to create this new layer of protection? Wasn't the Park Service doing a good job protecting America's scenic and natural treasures? Well, perhaps not, because Congress had also directed the Service to "promote . . . the use of the parks" and to provide for their "enjoyment" by the public. Thus were the men and women in the Smokey Bear hats torn between two conflicting missions: protection and use. And it wasn't even a toss-up. As an ever-increasing number of visitors and motor vehicles rushed to the parks in the postwar 1950s, the Park Service felt obliged to accommodate them.

Accommodation took the form of an ambitious program called Mission 66. Aiming to repair the park system's physical plant, which had deteriorated badly during the war years, Mission 66 (as in deadline for completion in 1966) delighted Capitol Hill. Congressmen, a Park Service director once noted, love to cut ribbons. Suddenly there was not only a dusting off of the older facilities but an unveiling of the new—new roads, new campgrounds, new visitor centers, new lodges and restaurants and housing for the employees of concessionaires.

Interior Secretary Stewart Udall was not altogether enamored of Mission 66, which he had inherited from his predecessor in the Eisenhower administration, or with the fact that while all this ribbon-cutting and ground-breaking had been going

Page 152: *Lichen-splattered granite boulders, dark ranks of spruce trees, and fog are trademarks of the rugged Maine coast. Such intimate moments await visitors to Acadia National Park, on Mount Desert Island. That is, if they escape the summer traffic jams on roads leading to the tourist mecca of Bar Harbor and to the usual photo-op stops in this small, fragmented, and unusually civilized national park. (Photo: Carr Clifton/Minden Pictures)*

Page 153, top: *Rising abruptly over a high basin known as Jackson Hole, the jagged peaks of Grand Teton National Park are possibly the most-photographed mountains in North America. (Photo: Carr Clifton/Minden Pictures)*

Page 153, bottom: *Autumn in Alaska's Denali National Park is brief but colorful as hardy quaking aspens and low-lying tundra shrubs shut down their pumping systems for winter. (Photo: Thomas D. Mangelsen)*

Bob Marshall, who helped found The Wilderness Society in 1935, was a charismatic figure in the environmental movement. A Forest Service colleague of Aldo Leopold, he was a prodigious hiker, sometimes covering seventy miles in a day. His 1930 article "The Problem of the Wilderness," which appeared in *Scientific Monthly*, was a seminal work in the formulation of a coherent national wilderness doctrine. "How many wilderness areas do we need?" Marshall was once asked. He replied, "How many Brahms symphonies do we need?"

Bob Marshall canoeing Minnesota's Quetico-Superior country in 1937. (The Wilderness Society)

on, no one seemed to have the foggiest idea of its impact on the natural resources that the parks were intended to protect. With the help of the National Academy of Sciences, Udall assembled a task force to examine these matters. And out of that study came a document called the Leopold Report, named for Chairman A. Starker Leopold of the University of California and son of Aldo Leopold. The report emphasized the ecological values of national parks, as distinct from the recreational. As a primary goal, it recommended that "the biotic associations within each park be maintained. . .as nearly as possible in the condition that prevailed when the area was first visited by the white man." A national park, it declared, "should represent a vignette of primitive America."

In 1964, George B. Hartzog Jr., a plain-speaking Carolinian, was selected by Udall to take over the directorship of the National Park Service. Hartzog faced two big challenges—first, the need to reverse the agency's deep-rooted inclination to turn some of the popular natural parks, such as Yosemite and Yellowstone, into romper rooms; and second, to take the pressure off those beleaguered places by acquiring new parklands, especially near the nation's major cities.

Buying real estate to make a national park was something Uncle Sam had never done before in any significant way. Heretofore, parks were either carved from the public domain (as in the case of Yellowstone), received through private philanthropy (as in the Rockefeller family gifts at Acadia and Grand Teton), or accepted as donations from the states (as in Great Smoky Mountains National Park, a gift from North Carolina and Tennessee). But now there was this newfangled trust called the Land and Water Conservation Fund, and Hartzog wasn't going to be abstemious about dipping into it.

There it was again—that confluence of fortunate and unpredictable circumstances: Udall, Hartzog, the Conservation Fund, and a Congress willing to put the money where its mouth was.

Among the first of the acquisitions was Cape Cod National Seashore, barely two hours from

Opposite: *Starfish cling to barnacle-encrusted rocks at low tide on Point Reyes National Seashore, north of San Francisco. A cattle-ranching peninsula with a stunningly varied coastline, Point Reyes was one of the National Park Service's great successes in preserving natural areas near major cities, using the Land and Water Conservation Fund. (Photo: Galen Rowell/ Mountain Light)*

Boston. Next, Point Reyes National Seashore, a skip and a jump north of San Francisco; Fire Island, a hop east from New York City; Padre Island, a getaway from San Antonio; the Indiana Dunes, a lunch-hour out of Chicago. And before the decade calendar could turn over a new leaf, Hartzog's people were already planning big urban parks even closer to the centers of major cities. In the seventies, those plans would result in New York City's Gateway National Recreation Area, San Francisco's Golden Gate NRA, a Cuyahoga Valley NRA linking Akron to Cleveland, and a Santa Monica Mountains NRA at the edge of Los Angeles.

But for all their efforts to bring recreation and open space to city people, Udall and Hartzog weren't about to neglect the need for more natural parks in the far country. In 1968, a torrent of new legislation flooded President Johnson's desk. Among the most notable results were the National Wild and Scenic Rivers System (now totalling some 10,000 riverine miles and ranging from the glacial Noatak in Alaska to the Southwest's turgid Rio Grande); a National Trails System (highlighted by the 2,000-mile Maine-to-Georgia Appalachian Trail); and designation of a North Cascades National Park in Washington State with two huge national recreation areas abutting it like bookends. Finally, after much acrimonious debate that often pitted one constituency of tree-huggers against another, a Redwood National Park was established in Northern California.

Designating new parks was only half the leitmotif of the 1960s, and the easier half at that. The harder part was defending parks already existing, more often than not from technological abuse. Consider, for example, the decade's most memorable issues—the proposed damming of the Grand Canyon and the engineered mischief that almost destroyed Everglades National Park. In both places, the stakes boiled down to a war over water.

Conservationists have crusaded against dams for almost as many years as they have been hugging trees. First was the dam at Hetch Hetchy, which flooded one of Yosemite's sacred valleys in 1913. Score one for the dam-builders. Then, in the 1950s, came plans for the Echo Park Dam in Utah's Dinosaur National Monument. The conservation community rallied to stop it; score one for their side. But score two for the dam-builders because, in lieu of Echo, they blocked the Colorado River at Glen Canyon. The Glen, however, wasn't dam enough for the Bureau of Reclamation. So in the mid-1960s, the Bureau decided to turn the Grand Canyon into a reservoir that would water the ranches and ranchettes of the Central Arizona Project. When conservationists complained that a reservoir would drown the canyon's world-class geologic strata, some Bureau panjandrum responded to the contrary; a reservoir, he said, would enable visitors in motorboats to actually touch the

Right: *Colorado River water jets from outlets at the bottom of Glen Canyon Dam. While the 710-foot-high dam is an engineering marvel and Lake Powell, with 1,900 miles of scenic shoreline, is a boating paradise, conservationists still decry the loss of an untamed Glen Canyon, memorialized by photographer Eliot Porter in a Sierra Club book,* The Place No One Knew. *(Photo: Tom Bean)*

Pages 158-159: *While the Sierra Club led the charge against Grand Canyon dams, the National Audubon Society rallied its forces to block a nightmarish scheme by the Dade County Port Authority to build the world's largest international jetport and "one of the great population centers of America" in the middle of the Everglades. The nail in the plan's coffin was a study by the U.S. Geological Survey that said the plan would destroy Everglades National Park. Subsequently, bald cypresses stand in the 729,000-acre Big Cypress National Preserve, set aside in the area coveted by the developers. (Photo: John Shaw)*

ancient rock, otherwise accessible only to cliff nesting swallows. Hearing that, the Sierra Club's charismatic David Brower uncorked a riposte, a full-page ad in *The New York Times.* "Should we also flood the Sistine Chapel," the ad inquired, "so the tourists can get nearer the ceiling?"

That ad and others like it cost the Sierra Club its tax-exempt status. But the Club's effective lobbying killed the dam.

While Sierrans stood watch at the Grand Canyon, the National Audubon Society was girding for a donnybrook in South Florida, where all kinds of ecological hell seemed ready to consume the nation's premiere subtropical park. The Everglades, and the Big Cypress Swamp next door, had been Audubon country ever since the Society first bloodied its nose shutting down the plume trade at the turn of the century. Now the Society was obliged to deal with a different problem—the quality and quantity of water flowing south down the Everglades' river of grass.

Floridians had long tampered with nature's plumbing system in the belief that drainage canals could turn the sawgrass prairies south of Lake Okeechobee into a Garden of Eden. Rid of the water, the rich glades muck was perfect for sugarcane and beans and tomatoes. And soon the farms were followed by little cities. In 1926 and again two years later, hurricanes swept Okeechobee over its banks. More than 2,000 people perished in the floods. Something had to be done. And, by and by, the U.S. Army Corps of Engineers would do it. The name of the game was the Central and South Florida Flood Control Project, a massive grid of more canals, more dikes, and more floodgates. In the dry season, the gates were shut to store up the water for use by the farmers and city folks. In the wet season, the gates were opened to flush high water out of the canefields.

At the downstream end of this plumbing system sat the newly dedicated Everglades National

The American crocodile is a rarely encountered denizen of saltwater areas in Everglades National Park, notably the mangrove keys of Florida Bay, which are uninhabited except for colonies of herons, spoonbills, pelicans, nesting eagles, and ospreys. The ubiquitous alligator, on the other hand, is largely confined to freshwater habitats. (Photo: Joe McDonald)

Park, a place of alligators and wading birds. But when the floodgates were shut, some birds and gators would perish for lack of water. And when the gates were open, other creatures would perish from too much—or be sickened by chemicals flushed from the growers' fields.

Ah, the Everglades. Some wag once likened its ups and downs to the Perils of Pauline. For no sooner had the Corps agreed under pressure to amend its destructive schedule of water releases than a new threat loomed on the very edge of the national park. The year was 1969 and the Dade County Port Authority was thinking big. Real big, as in a huge international jetport, the biggest in the world, with industries and think tanks and residential communities such that a Port Authoritarian would envision "one of the great population centers of America" rising over the cypress and the sawgrass.

But Dade's speeding train never quite got down the track to the trussed Pauline of Everglades Park. With Audubon's Charlie Callison sounding the alarm in his *National Outlook* magazine column and on Capitol Hill, and Society President Elvis Stahr rallying a national coalition to the barricades, the jetport scheme began to lose momentum. Finally, another Leopold report—this one by Aldo's other son, Luna, senior hydrologist of the U.S. Geological Survey—found that the Port Authority's plan would "inexorably destroy the South Florida ecosystem and thus Everglades National Park" by producing four

Sitting at an elevation of 6,384 feet in California's Sierra Nevada, Mono Lake is the last remnant of a body of water that once stretched from the glaciers of the Sierra to what is now the Nevada state line. Though landlocked, Mono Lake's waters are salty and rich in brine shrimp, brine flies, and a seasonal population of a million birds that feast upon them—including California gulls, eared grebes, avocets, two species of phalaropes, and a variety of ducks.

But perhaps the most unusual aspect of this lake is its tufa towers. Thousands of years ago, freshwater springs started to bubble up from the bottom of the lake, their calcium-rich waters mingling with the lake's carbonates. The residues accreted into clusters of tapering mounds. Hundreds of these exposed mounds ornament the banks and shallows of the lake today, forming an eerie, fairy tale architecture.

Ironically, these spires were revealed by the Los Angeles Department of Water and Power. In the 1930s, the department began tapping into the lake's freshwater tributaries to satisfy the water needs of the burgeoning Los Angeles basin, 300 miles to the south. As the lake shrank, more and more of the intriguing towers emerged. But by the end of the 1970s, the lake's salts and other natural chemicals became so concentrated that the lake's fragile ecosystem threatened to collapse. Concerned local citizens joined to form the Mono Lake Committee. Backed by California chapters of the National Audubon Society and other groups, they launched a legal and public relations campaign to stem the flow.

And they won. In 1994 the state of California ordered that the surface of Mono Lake be returned to an elevation of 6,392 feet—twenty feet above its historic low—and kept there. The state is expected to issue a final planning decision in October 1999; restoration will begin in the spring of 2000. Mono Lake may thus return to a level that will sustain its delicate, surreal balance of life. **—T. H. WATKINS**

Pages 162-163: *The moose was nearly extirpated from forests south of Canada by 1900. But today, close encounters with the world's largest deer are fairly predictable in the backcountry of northern national parks and wilderness areas. During the fall rut, however, it's best not to test the tolerance of a thousand-pound bull moose. (Photo: Thomas D. Mangelsen)*

million gallons of raw sewage each day and some 10,000 tons of jet-engine pollutants annually. Whereupon the federal government ruled there would be no big jetport complex at the edge of the park.

As the 1960s dwindled, who then could have guessed the times and changes awaiting the Everglades over the next thirty years? Now, three decades later, we wait for the latest 'Glades twist to unravel. But it is a promising twist: an $8 billion, twenty-year-long federal-state effort to restore ecological stability to the South Florida ecosystem. In an interview with *The New York Times*, Stuart Strahl, director of the National Audubon Society's Everglades office, described the project as "a test case of our interest in living sustainably with a natural ecosystem." And that was important, he said, because there is no other ecosystem like the Everglades anywhere in the world.

Once upon a time I lived at the edge of a wetland altogether different from the Everglades, a red maple swamp in southern Connecticut. Lonetown Marsh, they called it, though that was a misnomer because it is a swamp, maple snags in the shallows and clearwater holes in the deep defining it so. Seven acres, maybe eight. Snapping turtles and herons and mallards and wood ducks. Rosy dawns and golden sunsets. For more than fifteen years I cherished that view. Cherish the memory of it still, though it never really belonged just to me. The swamp belongs to

everyone. It is a natural area, a sanctuary, a piece of the public commons that might have been drained and developed as a shopping center had it not been for a couple of those fortunate circumstances of the 1960s. Namely, the aforementioned Land and Water Conservation Fund, and the landsaving it would inspire beyond the big national parks and wilderness areas, down among the grassroots of America.

As originally structured, the fund was set up to split its annual allocations more or less evenly between federal land acquisitions, such as Redwood National Park, and the states, which in turn would apportion a share to their municipalities. Like many small communities across the country, my town in Connecticut went after its share; in fact, probably got more than its share because, by the mid-1970s, it had squirreled away nearly a thousand acres of protected open space, including those seven acres athwart Lonetown Marsh.

In the course of some thirty years, the non-federal side of the Conservation Fund has invested more than $3 billion in state and local open space and outdoor recreation projects, assisting the development of small parks, trails, and natural areas in every state and, in aggregate, protecting an area larger than Delaware and Rhode Island combined. This is surely one of the greatest legacies from the 1960s, yet few Americans are aware of it. Fewer still are aware of how successive administrations and Congresses since the early 1980s have either robbed the fund to pay down the national debt or simply refused to appropriate the authorized monies. The 1960s were never like this.

They weren't meant to be. We are lucky to have what we have. Magnificent national parks. Wilderness areas high, wide, and handsome. Canyons and swamps with vigilant guardians. Little spaces such as Lonetown Marsh. There will be more to come. There has to be. The confluence of unpredictable circumstances absolutely guarantees it.

1970

The Shadow of Extinction

1970

The Shadow of Extinction

by George Laycock

BY THE 1970s, conservationists had realized that the list of North American wildlife approaching extinction was both long and frightening—generating momentum for the watershed Endangered Species Act of 1973. From the beginning, the arrival of Europeans in the New World was bad news for native animals. The first species in historic times to pay the ultimate price probably was Steller's sea cow, a blimplike creature discovered in Alaskan waters in 1741. No sooner had the first shipload of Russian explorers and fur-hunters seen the thirty-foot-long, three-and-one-half-ton beasts drifting about offshore than they figured out how to catch them. The primitive sea cows, relatives of the manatee, may have been disappearing from the Bering Sea for natural reasons, but hungry sailors accelerated their demise, eating them into extinction in just twenty-seven years.

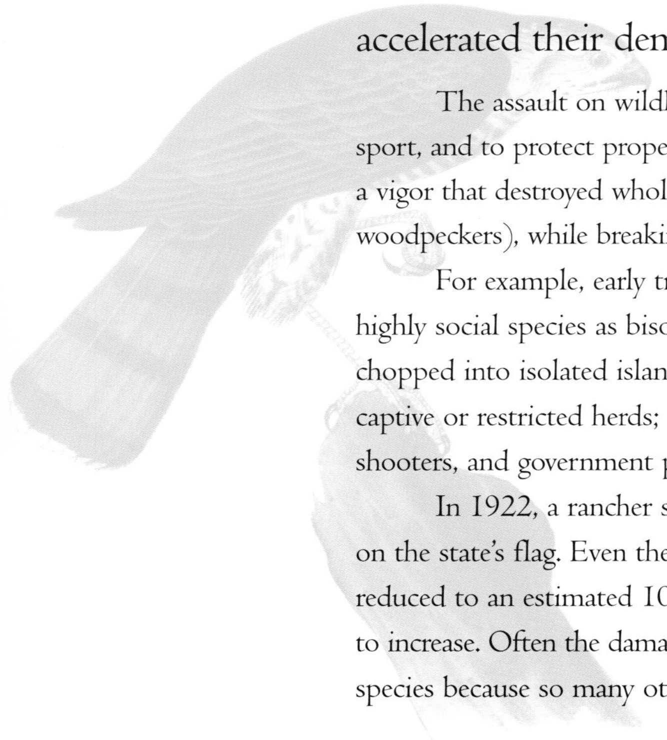

The assault on wildlife shifted into high gear during the 1800s as Americans killed animals relentlessly for food, sport, and to protect property such as livestock and crops. Settlers and exploiters also attacked the native landscape with a vigor that destroyed whole ecosystems, slashing away eastern forests (home to bears, deer, turkeys, grouse, and giant woodpeckers), while breaking up the western grasslands with plows, fences, livestock, and imported grasses and weeds.

For example, early travelers crossing the Great Plains met wildlife in numbers beyond counting, especially such highly social species as bison, prairie dogs, and prairie chickens. But over succeeding decades, the vast grasslands were chopped into isolated islands of habitat that grew smaller and smaller. As a result, the wild-spirited bison are reduced to captive or restricted herds; prairie chickens are gone or going; and black-tailed prairie dogs, still under attack by ranchers, shooters, and government poisoners, are proposed candidates for the official list of threatened and endangered species.

In 1922, a rancher shot the last known California grizzly bear, marking the end of a subspecies found today only on the state's flag. Even the ubiquitous pronghorn antelope, whose population once numbered 40 million or more, was reduced to an estimated 10,000 animals and extinction seemed a real possibility until protection allowed their numbers to increase. Often the damage didn't end with a single creature in trouble. The prairie dog is known to science as a keystone species because so many other animals are linked to it, including the kit fox, badger, black-footed ferret, burrowing owl,

and various hawks, plus rattlesnakes that take shelter in its subterranean lodgings.

Meanwhile, by the turn of the century Florida's most spectacular water birds were being sacrificed to decorate ladies' hats. In 1914, the last known passenger pigeon, a species that once numbered in the billions and may have been the world's most abundant bird, died in a zoo cage. Four years later, the flashy Carolina parakeet was down to a single listless individual in an adjoining cage, with little time left on Earth. In

Pages 164-165: *Dall sheep rams ruminate in a high meadow of Alaska's Brooks Range. Wild sheep inhabit rough, craggy terrain where there is an ample supply of grass, little competition for food from other ungulates such as deer, and places where ewes and lambs can escape from predators. Like the bighorn sheep of the Rockies, Dall sheep form bands segregrated by sex. A mature ewe will lead younger ewes and their lambs, while a ram that has earned top place in the hierarchy by winning head-butting contests will reign over as many as a dozen other males. (Photo: Thomas D. Mangelsen)*

Page 167: *Black bear cubs, born helpless and hairless around the end of January, leave the winter den with their mother in April and stay with her until the following spring. While the usual litter size is two, it's not unusual to see triplets, like these cubs climbing a white pine in Seney National Wildlife Refuge in Michigan's Upper Peninsula. (Photo: Carl R. Sams II)*

Right: *No one knows when the Carolina parakeet passed into extinction. The last captive bird died in a cage at the Cincinnati Zoo in 1918. By then, the large flocks that ranged across eastern North America, from New York and the Great Lakes to the Gulf of Mexico, were ancient history. North America's only native parrot fed on the seeds of various wild plants, as in this portrait by Audubon, but the species was doomed when the birds turned their attention to fruit crops. Reputable scientists believed they spotted a small party of yellow-headed parakeets in a South Carolina swamp as late as 1936, but the sighting was never confirmed. (Photo: Library of Congress)*

Opposite: *A badger dines on scrambled mallard eggs. The badger's head, with its white striping and black sideburns, is wedge-shaped for nosing into the holes of burrowing rodents ranging in size from deer mice to woodchucks. A keen sense of smell tells it whether anyone is home; and before excavating a ground squirrel family's den, a badger typically plugs all but one entrance. Thanks to thick fur and loose skin, a badger can turn around with amazing ease in a tight burrow. And a nictitating membrane protects its eyes from flying dirt. (Photo: Michael Quinton/Minden Pictures)*

the mid-1930s, National Audubon Society biologist James T. Tanner, searching southern swamps that were being logged for their ancient trees, saw his last ivory-billed woodpecker. And the towering whooping crane, traveling south from its wilderness breeding grounds in northern Canada to spend the winter stalking crabs on the Texas coast, declined to fewer than twenty birds.

Perhaps the best known of all the vanishing birds in this century is the bald eagle, our national symbol and the species that Canadian Charles L. Broley adopted in 1942. Broley was newly retired from his bank manager's job and en route to Florida, where he intended to loaf in the sun and pursue his birdwatching hobby. He stopped in Washington, D.C., to visit with National Audubon Society staff member Richard H. Pough, who explained to Broley that he was deeply concerned about the bald eagle. Florida developers were cutting down eagle nest trees while country boys were climbing to the eyries and stealing the eggs, which they peddled to collectors at $10 a clutch. Also, as Pough explained, scientists didn't understand the eagles' seasonal migration patterns. He suggested bird study with a purpose: Instead of simply watching and listing birds, could Broley begin banding eagles? Pough handed him four eagle-size leg bands and promised more as needed.

Rather than hire boys to do his climbing, the sixty-year-old Broley, small in stature but long on energy, ascended the towering nest trees himself. He devised an ingenious system of rope ladders and hooks and pulled himself into the treetops. There, 100 feet above the ground, he would clamber over the rim of the huge stick nest into the middle of a clutch of hissing eaglets. In a dozen years, Broley banded 1,200 young eagles, more than all others combined had ever banded, and recoveries of the numbered aluminum rings began to reveal patterns in the eagle's post-breeding travels.

Then came years of plummeting eagle populations. Adult birds were no longer raising enough offspring to replace themselves. In 1958, instead of the 125 to 150 young eagles he had banded in earlier years, Broley found only one, and by the 1960s eagle numbers south of the Canadian border had fallen to 400 breeding pairs. Research showed that DDE, a metabolite of DDT, was accumulating in the fatty tissues not only of eagles but also of pelicans and peregrine falcons, causing them to lay eggs with shells so thin they broke under the weight of the incubating birds.

By then, extinction had claimed twenty-eight species of North American birds, sixteen mammals, and twelve fishes. Extinction, of course, is a natural phenomenon. Scientists know there were times of abnormally high rates of extinction long before man walked the Earth. Paleontologists deciphering fossil

Right and far right: *A backhoe digs a decorative lake for a new development in the Florida Everglades, while the suburbs eat farmland near Portland, Oregon. Habitat destruction is today's major threat to native wildlife. (Photos: Gary Braasch)*

Opposite: *The salmon are spawning, and bald eagles congregate in a towering spruce along a river on the Northwest coast where there is plenty of room for the majestic birds. That's not the case in more populated parts of their range. Bald eagles avoid human company. Yet at a time when the species is recovering nicely from the DDT blight that once threatened its existence south of the Canadian border, habitat in important areas like Chesapeake Bay is being lost to accelerating housing and recreation development on the Virginia and Maryland shores. (Photo: Thomas D. Mangelsen)*

Pages 172-173: *Fairy terns on Midway Island at the far end of the Hawaiian chain. Other terns nest on beaches, but this pure-white bird is unique in that it lays and incubates a single egg on the slender branch of a tree or shrub. (Photo: Daniel J. Cox/Natural Exposures)*

records have identified five such periods, one of which erased the dinosaurs. But the world is now caught up in a modern mass extinction that makes those prehistoric ones look like practice sessions. The calculations of Rutgers University biology professor David Ehrenfeld indicate that Earth is losing mammal species a thousand times faster than it did during the ice ages of the Pleistocene Epoch. A report from the National Science Board calls the current spasm of extinction "the most catastrophic loss of species in the last 65 million years."

In the 1800s, wildlife populations were often decimated by unregulated hunting, especially for the commercial food and millinery markets. But the causes changed over time. As Paul and Anne Ehrlich wrote in their excellent book, *Extinction*, "Change in either the physical or biological environment is the key to extinction." One comprehensive study of human impact on wildlife, as recently reported by David S. Wilcove in the journal, *BioScience*, rates habitat destruction as the leading threat to native wildlife. A partial list of the forces at work includes agriculture, mining, commercial development, deforestation, dams, disease, oil and gas extraction, pesticides, off-road vehicles, siltation, towers and transmission lines, and wetland drainage.

Habitat destruction as an agent of extinction is followed closely by the introduction of exotic plants and animals that alter habitat, compete for nest sites and food, hybridize with or prey on native species, and carry disease. Estimates place the number of alien species that have become established in the United States at 4,500 and they figure into the troubles of nearly half of the country's endangered species. Once established, these invaders are usually impossible to eliminate. Starlings, carp, and dandelions, to name just three, are here to stay.

Islands, isolated and limited in size, are especially vulnerable. Of seventy known species and subspecies of Hawaiian birds, twenty-four are gone and thirty more are listed as endangered or threatened. When Captain Cook first arrived in the Hawaiian

Islands he must have believed that only good would come from his gift of goats to the chiefs. Set free, the agile and adaptable goats established vigorous permanent populations that destroyed native plants and caused serious erosion. Between 1930 and 1970 the National Park Service eliminated 70,000 goats from Hawaii Volcanoes National Park, then conducted an aerial census to see what it had accomplished. The park still had 15,000 goats, about the same number as when the control program was begun. Nothing short of a costly goat-proof fence around the park and constant vigilance would slow the destruction.

On one Audubon assignment, I accompanied U.S. Fish and Wildlife Service endangered species ecologist John Sincock into the mysterious Alakai Swamp, measuring some ten miles long by three wide, on a Kauai mountaintop. After we made camp, John and I headed off into the tangled vegetation, searching for what was the world's rarest bird. We had gone but a short distance when he stopped to listen. "That's the O'o," he said. We moved closer until we could see the bird flitting about in the ohia lehua trees. It was about the size of a catbird and in the shadows it appeared dark, either black or brown, but with brilliant yellow feathers on the legs.

The Kauai O'o had gone downhill fast. Ornithologist George C. Munro, who studied Hawaii's avifauna for half a century, said that prior to 1900 the O'o was abundant on Kauai. Yet the bird we were watching may have been the last of its kind. In clear, melodious tones, it sang an ancient solo over and over to a mate that never answered. The O'o's troubles probably began when early sailing vessels arrived in Hawaii and their crews came ashore for fresh water. Rinsing their kegs in the streams, the sailors probably washed out larvae of the first tropical mosquitoes to reach Hawaii. Biologists now know these mosquitoes carried avian malaria from poultry to native birds that had not evolved in the presence of

Most of the wonderfully varied Hawaiian honeycreepers that evolved from a single finch ancestor are extinct or endangered. But the scarlet-and-black iiwi is common on the islands of Hawaii, Maui, and Kauai, where it uses a sickle-shaped bill to drink nectar from the flowers of native trees like the ohia lehua and an assortment of introduced tropical plants. (Photo: Frans Lanting/ Minden Pictures)

the disease and had little resistance to it. The O'o is only one of its victims.

Then there are gone-wild pigs, self-propelled rototillers that rummage the Hawaiian forest floor for birds, eggs, and roots; rats that came ashore with early sailors; and on some islands, descendants of the mongooses that were released in a futile effort to control the rats in sugar canefields. The mongoose eats anything from beetles to birds' eggs.

Northwest of Hawaii's main islands, within the Hawaiian Islands National Wildlife Refuge, lies a string of smaller uninhabited islands, one every hundred miles or so. On another assignment, I traveled with U.S. Fish and Wildlife Service biologists on their annual inspection of this refuge. We sailed aboard a Coast Guard cutter whose crew put us ashore, often with difficulty, and nearly everywhere we went there were endangered species ranging from finches to monk seals. Our longest stop was on Laysan, a low-lying island where guano miners arrived in 1890. Innocently enough, the miners sent for a few domestic rabbits and turned them loose in the bushes to fend for themselves and serve as a self-renewing source of fresh meat.

The rabbits, alas, renewed themselves to excess, and years later government workers had to come to the now abandoned island to shoot or trap them by the thousands. But by the time they were eradicated, the rabbits had decimated the native plantlife and hastened extinction of three of Laysan's endemic birds—the wren-sized Laysan millerbird, a small flightless rail, and the Laysan honeycreeper.

A more recent invader that threatens Hawaii's

The brown tree snake, a tree-climbing constrictor that attains a length of eight feet, exterminated most of Guam's endemic birdlife after it reached the island on a U.S. Navy ship at the end of World War II. The snake is a notorious stowaway and at Hawaii's Honolulu airport, trained beagles are used to check planes, freight, and baggage arriving from Guam. (Photo: John Mitchell/ Photo Researchers)

remnant native wildlife is the brown tree snake, which sometimes arrives aboard commercial airliners. The tree-climbing snake reached Guam in the 1940s, hiding in World War II military equipment, and efforts to control it have cost millions of dollars, with no end in sight. Growing to a length of eight feet, the brown tree snake frequently crawls across power lines and in one year caused 200 major blackouts. Nine of twelve native forest birds on Guam are gone because of the brown tree snake and the other three are dwindling. So at the Honolulu airport, trained beagles scamper around incoming baggage and freight from Guam, searching for snakes while uneasy biologists wonder how many of them are eluding the inspectors.

Along with all the wild animals on the official federal list of threatened and endangered species are native plants ranging from the silversword on Maui to the Furbish lousewort of Maine. South Florida, plagued by everything from free-ranging boa constrictors to piranhas, is also being swallowed by foreign plants that crowd out native vegetation. Mats of hydrilla, originally imported for use in aquariums, clog waterways, and the state spends millions of dollars a year in endless control efforts. Melaleuca, brought from Australia as an ornamental tree, poisons other plants, dries up wetlands, and forms dense thickets that displace native wildlife. The U.S. Department of Agriculture places the annual loss to alien plants in the billions of dollars. For example, spotted knapweed has crowded out millions of acres of native grass on western rangelands.

Over broad areas of the country, shallow wetlands are being smothered by stands of purple loosestrife, a pretty but pernicious alien that chokes out the native marsh plants on which waterfowl depend. Loosestrife accomplishes this because it is allelopathic, which means it produces a toxin that suppresses other plants and reduces competition. The purple monoculture becomes a wildlife barrenland. Other costly

botanical mistakes include kudzu, "the vine that ate the South," and multiflora rose, that forms impenetrable thorny jungles. Both plants were promoted by the U.S. Department of Agriculture, telling landowners that kudzu would control erosion and multiflora rose would create low cost living fences.

Unintentional introductions, meanwhile, have proved devastating. Many native trees, unable to adapt to alien insects and pathogens, are dying off. The American chestnut, once the dominant tree in Appalachian forests where its rich nuts fed bears, deer, turkeys and squirrels, is gone. Elegant American elms vanished from village streets. Both fell victim to foreign fungi. In his book *The Dying of the Trees,* conservationist Charles E. Little lists other species that are now in serious trouble, mostly from combinations of air pollution (especially acid rain) and exotic organisms. Among them are the white ash, butternut, dogwood, sugar maple, American beech, and hemlock. On top of Clingman's Dome, highest peak in the Great Smoky Mountains National Park in Gatlinburg, Tennessee, stands a forest of Fraser firs as naked as utility poles. The firs died because the balsam woolly adelgid, a sucking aphidlike insect light enough to be carried on the wind, reached the United States on nursery stock from Europe.

And trouble is brewing beneath the surface of North American lakes and streams. A recent U.S. Fish and Wildlife Service publication lists 116 native fish as either endangered or threatened. Many of

Purple loosestrife is a pretty but pernicious weed that has choked wetland habitats across North America. Botanists believe the plant reached North America from Europe in the early 1800s by two routes: seeds buried in ships' ballast that was dumped on the shore at Northeast ports, and plants imported for medicinal and ornamental purposes. Purple loosestrife spread along waterways and roadside drainage ditches and now covers hundreds of thousands of acres, but the introduction of beetles that are the plant's natural enemies may reverse the tide. (Photo: John Shaw)

In 1992, after ten years of campaigning by the local community, Congress created the Monterey Bay National Marine Sanctuary. Encompassing more than 5,300 square miles of the Pacific Ocean and California's shoreline, it is the nation's largest marine sanctuary and four times as large as Yosemite National Park. Julie Packard, a founder of the nearby Monterey Bay Aquarium and a proponent of the sanctuary's creation, has called it "one of the most significant conservation achievements of the 1990s."

Monterey Bay has wetlands, rocky shores, and the nation's biggest expanse of giant kelp forest. Above all, it contains the "Grand Canyon of the Pacific Coast"—Monterey Canyon, an underwater gorge thousands of feet deep that comes within a mile of the shore. The canyon's nutrient-rich waters help sustain sea otters and a variety of other wildlife.

At Point Año Nuevo, one of the many sandy beaches in the sanctuary, immense elephant seals bellow in their breeding rookery. They are just one of twenty-eight species of mammals that call the bay home. Its 100-plus bird species include pelicans, loons, grebes, and flocks of shearwaters that sometimes number in the tens of thousands. What's more, each year researchers discover dozens of new species—mostly invertebrates such as jellyfish—within the sanctuary.

With more than 350 miles of coastline and a boundary extending as far as 50 miles offshore, the sanctuary poses formidable management challenges. The potential for water pollution from an oil spill or from urban and agricultural runoff is a major concern. And restrictions on fishing and jet-skis have provoked heated controversies. "This is a destination for ten to fifteen million beachgoers each year," says the sanctuary's superintendent, William Douros. "The danger of it being loved to death is fairly high." —Carl Safina

them are in jeopardy because water quality has been degraded with chemicals, heat, and sediment. But fish also fall victim to introduced competitors. Walter R. Courtenay Jr., an authority on aquatic ecosystems at Florida Atlantic University, wrote in 1991: "There are 226 fish species established beyond their historic natural ranges of distribution as reproducing populations in waters of the continental United States, Hawaii and Puerto Rico." Eighty percent of these were introduced after 1950.

Yellowstone Lake, in the heart of our oldest national park, is known for its own subspecies of cutthroat trout—modest in size, beautifully colored, and a favorite of visiting anglers. But not long ago, someone illegally slipped lake trout into Yellowstone. Because these predators grow to twenty pounds or more by feeding on smaller fish, cutthroat trout included, scientists predict that the lake trout will reduce the cutthroat population by ninety percent. But the native trout are not the only species that will suffer. When the cutthroats swim up the lake's tributary

Right: *The beautiful cutthroat trout of Yellowstone Lake may disappear because anonymous sport fishermen introduced lake trout—which feed on smaller fish including cutthroats—to the cold, deep waters. (Photo: Michael Quinton/Minden Pictures)*

Opposite: *Brown pelicans make spectacular dives in pursuit of fish. Like bald eagles and peregrine falcons, pelicans also suffered from thin-shelled eggs due to pesticide residues in their prey. (Photo: Thomas D. Mangelsen)*

Above: *A bald eagle soars over a glacier-scarred Alaskan mountain. (Photo: Thomas D. Mangelsen)*

Pages 180-181: *A wide cleft in the Utah canyonlands is an easy leap for a powerful mountain lion. (Photo: Daniel J. Cox/ Natural Exposures)*

streams to spawn, a percentage of them becomes food for white pelicans, bald eagles, ospreys, otters, and grizzly bears. Lake trout, however, spawn in the lake's deep water.

According to Courtenay, biological pollution of North American waters began with the importation of goldfish in the 1600s. In 1887, Rudolph Hessel, acting on behalf of the United States government, returned from Europe escorting 345 carp to their home in the New World. Congressmen lined up to get their share of carp for eager constituents and before long this bottom-rooting fish, which turned out to be of poor eating quality and inferior as a sport fish, had permanently established itself across the country. Despite the potential environmental impact, state fisheries people still search for new species to keep anglers happy. Meanwhile, the pet trade imports millions of fish annually and several species have escaped and established free-swimming populations. And freighters dumping ballast from foreign ports have added to the Great Lakes a hodgepodge of invaders including the ruff, round goby, and the infamous zebra mussel. The latter is a a rampaging European bivalve that is spreading inland and threatening native mussels.

If there is a bright spot in the chronicle of extinction and near-extinction, it is found in the country's gradual awakening to the magnitude of the disaster. Inspired by the National Audubon Society's war on plume-hunters, Americans convinced politicians that they were serious about saving wildlife. Conservationists' efforts started to pay off in 1900 when Congress passed the Lacey Act, which made it a federal crime to ship illegally taken wildlife, including feathers for the plume trade, across state lines. President Theodore Roosevelt weighed in by creating a number of national wildlife refuges (now numbering more than 500). Over the years, several refuges were set aside specifically for endangered species: Red Rock Lakes in Montana for trumpeter swans, Attwater Prairie Chicken NWR in Texas, and the National Key Deer Refuge at the tip of Florida.

In 1966, Congress passed an Endangered Species Preservation Act that was toothless and underfunded. It was replaced three years later by the Endangered Species Conservation Act, which brought better funding and law enforcement to the effort, but protected only species facing imminent extinction. This shortcoming was corrected by the Endangered Species Act of 1973 and amendments that directed the U.S. Fish and Wildlife Service to list both endangered and threatened plants and animals along with their critical habitats, then work out plans to save them. The act is working. It has slowed the rate of extinction and reversed downward trends for some species, including the bald eagle. But by 1998, the list of species in trouble had grown to 902, and there were a great many candidates still to be studied for possible inclusion.

As the end of the twentieth century approached and the Endangered Species Act came up for renewal, it was needed more than ever.

1980

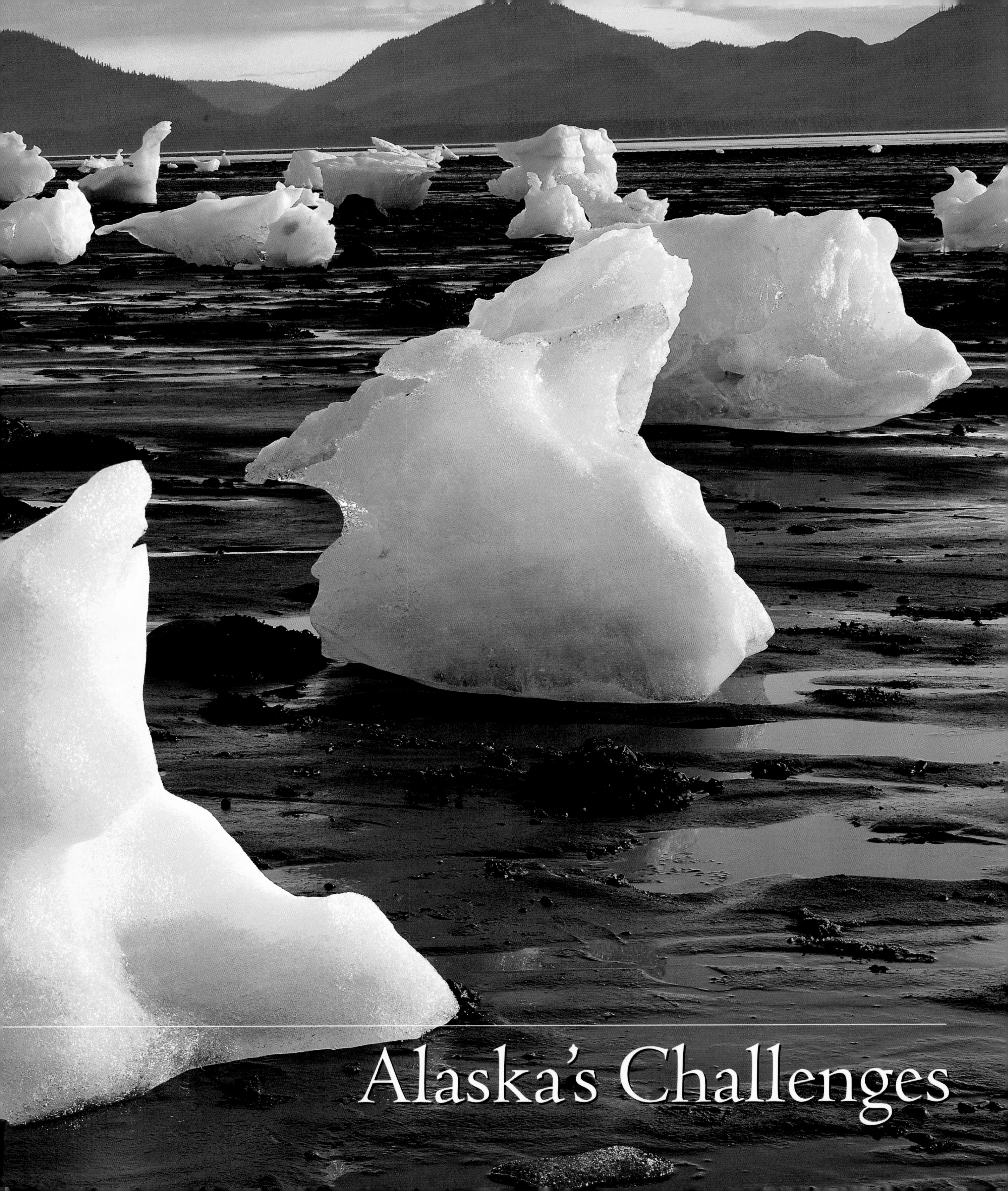

Alaska's Challenges

1980

Alaska's Challenges

by George Laycock

IN THE GRAY HALF-LIGHT OF THE ARCTIC EVENING we watch the pilot turn his single-engine plane into the wind. The aircraft gains speed until its aluminum pontoons are flanked by white walls of spray and, near the far side of the lake, it lifts smoothly from the cold, dark waters. The drone of the engine dies in the distance, leaving us alone in a wild setting as empty of human influence as it is possible to find today in all of North America.

There are no roads here in the heart of the Arctic National Wildlife Refuge, no wires, billboards, buildings, or sounds, except the whisper of the wind in the dwarf willows and the call of an Arctic loon from somewhere out on the lake. In this decade late in the twentieth century, *Audubon* editor, Les Line, and I have come to the northern edge of the continent to report back to members of the National Audubon Society on what America stands to lose if this preserve in Alaska's northeast corner is opened to development, as the oil industry would have it.

The decade began with a tour de force by the environmental community when Congress was persuaded to pass the Alaska National Interest Lands Conservation Act of 1980. When President Jimmy Carter signed the legislation into law, Americans celebrated what one Audubon Society official called "the single largest land conservation achievement in the nation's history." The act brought protection to 104 million acres—a California-sized treasury of lands in new national parks, refuges, forests, and conservation areas. But challenges remained in "The Great Land," as Alaska is sometimes called, and for conservationists the most troubling problem of all lay in the Arctic Refuge's northernmost section, where Les and I are headed.

The following day we are airlifted past glaciers and craggy peaks of the Brooks Range where pure-white Dall sheep stand precariously on narrow ledges, then down the North Slope and out across the coastal plain, land of grizzly bear, wolf, musk ox, and ptarmigan. My journal from an earlier trip, and my vivid memories, tell me that I once saw caribou 30,000 strong spread across the tundra. The caribou assemble every summer on this ancestral calving ground, where winds make the mosquitoes tolerable and where predators are visible from a distance.

After visits with Alaska biologists who track the caribou through the seasons, I told *Audubon* readers that the Porcupine herd divides its time between the United States and Canada. "In summer," I wrote, "the cows come over the mountains into Alaska, streaming down onto the broad, greening Arctic plain in steaming, grunting, belching mobs, and there they drop their new crop of calves. The bulls and barren cows, moving more leisurely, arrive later." Then, ahead of

Left: *Dall sheep lambs are precocial and able to climb as well as their mothers a day or two after their birth. By their second spring, they are totally independent of their parents. But while young males will wander off and eventually attach themselves to a band of older rams, the young females remain with an all-ewe herd that often is an expanded family group. (Photo: Daniel J. Cox/Natural Exposures)*

Below: *A musk-oxen herd's unique defense formation evolved as a way to protect the animals' vulnerable hindquarters (as well as calves) from marauding wolves. The dominant bull will stand to the side of the circle, making sure that other musk-oxen stay in the formation and charging the predator with its bony, horn-armed helmet. (Photo: Art Wolfe)*

Pages 182-183: At low tide, a fjord in the Stikine-Leconte Wilderness in southeast Alaska's Tongass National Forest is covered with icebergs from a calving glacier. The largest of America's more than 150 national forests, the Tongass presides over nearly 17 million acres of ancient temperate rain forest, hundreds of islands, glacier-carved peaks, and when the salmon are spawning, the world's greatest concentrations of bald eagles and brown bears. For years, the Tongass has been a battleground for the U.S. Forest Service's logging policies, which allowed giant spruce and hemlock trees to be sold to mills for the price of a hamburger. (Photo: Carr Clifton/Minden Pictures)

Page 185: While the habitat of this bull caribou in Alaska's Denali National Park is secure, a dark, oily cloud hangs over the coastal plain of the Arctic National Wildlife Refuge—the birthing area for caribou cows from the famous Porcupine herd. The oil industry, having tapped the reservoirs of Prudhoe Bay to the west, believe more riches lie beneath refuge lands where breezes off the Arctic Ocean provide 150,000 migrant caribou with relief from hordes of mosquitoes and biting flies. Conservationists, led by the National Audubon Society, have blocked the drilling rigs but the fight is far from resolved. (Photo: Art Wolfe)

winter, which comes early in this North Country, the restless herd flows up and down the river valleys, returning to the forests of Canada's Yukon Territory.

The caribou of the famed Porcupine herd, numbering some 150,000 animals, are long-distance travelers: twice a year they walk and trot hundreds of miles between birthing area and wintering grounds in a spectacle that is rivaled only by the migration of big ungulates on the Serengeti Plains of East Africa. But this is a toll road for caribou, for they are escorted by wolves, symbols of the Arctic and tokens of the wilderness.

When you walk on the tundra, you seldom see or hear the wolf, but it is close to the surface of the mind. "The world needs a place," wrote Robert Weeden, prominent Alaskan educator and conservationist, "where wolves stalk the strandlines in the dark, because a land that can produce a wolf is a healthy, robust, and perfect land." Every night we listen for the wild song of the wolf, but none calls within our hearing. The mighty grizzly bear is also here to take a tariff from the caribou. Hunter and hunted, all are associates in a working ecosystem forged over the ages.

The national wildlife refuge on which the caribou and dozens of other wild species depend covers 19 million acres. From its southern boundary 200 miles north of Fairbanks it stretches northward another 150 miles to the Beaufort Sea. Permanent sheets of ice beneath the tundra form impervious barriers, and in summer water from melting snow and ice stays on the surface in countless shimmering ponds and rivulets and turns the tundra soggy. These are the breeding places for hordes of mosquitoes and other insects that provide the food base which draws seasonal residents to the year-round home of brown bears, Arctic foxes, lemmings, and ground squirrels. In winter you might see only ravens and ptarmigan here, but in summer the Arctic is reborn as migratory birds return from wintering places in the southern states and in Central and South America. A few even fly in from Asia and Africa.

Right: The Arctic fox's luxurious winter coat protects this little canid from life-numbing cold as it roams the pack ice in the company of polar bears, eating leftovers from seal kills. In summer, the foxes prey on birds' eggs and lemmings, when these cyclical rodents are abundant. One pair of Arctic foxes and their pups consumed 1,800 lemmings during the three-month denning period. (Photo: Art Wolfe)

Dainty shorebirds—sandpipers, whimbrels, wandering tattlers, dunlins, and others—step about on spindly legs, gathering energy as they feast on invertebrates. Eiders, oldsquaws, pintails, brant, and other waterfowl pass back and forth while songbirds tend their hidden nests in the tundra grasses. In all, seventy-four species of birds return to the Arctic National Wildlife Refuge each summer to raise their young. They are birds in a hurry because this northern land is usually snow-free only between the first week of June and early September.

In early spring, the tundra swans also arrive to establish nesting territories—or reclaim old ones—near the edge of ponds where the aquatic plants they eat are abundant. The great white birds arrive from wintering areas along the East Coast after pulling their twenty-pound bodies through the sky for thousands of miles. On my first visit to this refuge, I flew with Ave Thayer, the lanky, soft-spoken manager whose

office was in Fairbanks but who spent as much time as possible on his refuge. Flying a mile high, Ave easily counted the swans that had subdivided the coast of the Beaufort Sea into territories with a nest every mile or so. With each pair of brilliant white swans were their gray cygnets, the young of the year, that would soon travel with their parents on their maiden migration to wintering places on Chesapeake Bay.

It is important that Les and I get the message across to *Audubon* readers that there is more at stake in the Arctic National Wildlife Refuge fight than caribou. Oil company representatives, hoping to limit debate to a single species, say that with improved technology they can drill for the oil without upsetting the age-old routine of the caribou. Ecologists doubt this and explain that even if the industry's claim is true, it is the answer to the wrong question and no comfort because caribou are but one part of a highly sensitive complex of Arctic plants and animals.

Furthermore, there is no guarantee that the industry can find enough oil beneath the coastal plain of the Arctic Refuge to economically justify sacrificing it. Official studies place the probability at 19 percent—providing the oil brings $30 a barrel. Two decades later as I write this, the price of North Slope crude, according to *The Wall Street Journal*, is less than half that price. But the oil industry still hopes to invade a wilderness refuge where vehicle tracks on the tundra become scar tissue that lasts a century or more.

For Dave Cline, the National Audubon Society's representative in Alaska in the eighties, the fate of the Arctic National Wildlife Refuge was his primary concern. But Dave was also watchdogging the four-foot diameter steel pipe that carries Prudhoe Bay crude oil south nearly 800 miles to the ice-free port of Valdez, and the 400-mile-long Haul Road that parallels the northern half of the pipeline like a giant tapeworm. On one *Audubon* assignment I accompanied Dave and a team of state employees the entire length of the Haul Road. Giant trucks, creating individual dust storms, ran with lights on full time. We saw almost no wildlife, and Dave agreed with me that it was a long, boring trip. The debate then was whether to lift restrictions on public use of the Haul Road north of the Yukon River. The road has since been thrown open to the public and tour buses run to Prudhoe Bay.

When Prudhoe Bay crude oil reaches the end of the pipeline in Valdez, it is transferred to storage tanks, then loaded onto huge oceangoing tankers. From the earliest days of this transport system, conservationists saw it as the mother of disaster. Citizens in the scenic fishing village of Cordova, and others, argued that the pipeline should carry oil to the Midwest instead of the environmentally sensitive Valdez area. *Audubon* warned in 1977 that the oilport was "hazardous beyond belief." Tragedy was predictable. The only question was when.

Disaster struck twelve years later and I was on my way back to Alaska to report on the pandemonium spawned when one of the world's largest tankers, a ship

Pages 188-189: *Top predators of the High Arctic, polar bears concentrate on drifting pack ice in the summer, feeding mainly on ringed seals. As the long winter sets in, a female bear will leave the ice for shore to dig a maternity den in the snow. With as many as three cubs in tow, the sow will break her way out of the chamber in late March. (Photo: Thomas D. Mangelsen)*

Opposite: *The old squaw drake, with its streaming central tail feathers and striking black-and-chestnut plumage, waits for ice to melt on its tundra breeding pond. (Photo: Art Morris/Birds As Art)*

Left: *A tundra swan guards four newly hatched cygnets at her nest on the Yukon Delta National Wildlife Refuge. About the size of the state of Indiana, this refuge on the Bering Sea coast is literally filled with nesting birds during the short Arctic summer, including most of the continent's tundra swan population. Other summer residents include shorebirds like the rare bristle-thighed curlew that spend the winter as far away as Australia, and unimaginable numbers of small songbirds like the Lapland longspur. (Photo: Stephen J. Krasemann/Photo Researchers)*

as long as three football fields, flushed 11 million gallons of North Slope crude oil into the fertile waters of Prince William Sound. I reported to *Audubon* readers that, "Shortly past midnight, on March 24, 1989, twenty-five miles from the terminal, the *Exxon Valdez* had veered some two miles off course. The layer of water separating her hull from the rocks grew thinner. Her bow was now plowing through the darkness, aimed directly at Bligh Reef, one of the best-known shipping hazards in Prince William Sound. The water waiting for her on Bligh Reef was less than forty feet deep—in some places much less." The reef became a giant can opener, slashing the hull of the supertanker. That's where I first saw her as we flew in low across the sound toward our landing in Anchorage.

There followed, over the coming months, the most costly oil cleanup effort ever attempted, but the wild animals still died by the thousands. Dave Cline reported to National Audubon Society president, Peter Berle, "Anyone who cares about wildlife would be sickened by what I have seen: hundreds of dead birds, their plumage blackened by thick oil, which destroys the thermal insulation, causing them to die of shock and hypothermia." Rescue workers picked up 36,000 seabirds of several species while biologists on the scene estimated that in excess of 300,000

North of Fairbanks, the 400-mile Haul Road parallels the four-foot-diameter pipeline that carries North Slope crude oil to the ice-free port of Valdez. Tour buses now run to Prudhoe Bay. (Photo: Natalie B. Fobes)

Right and far right: Rescuers attempt to clean a cormorant after the Exxon Valdez oil spill that killed 300,000 birds in the spring of 1989, along with this sea otter and a thousand others of its kind. (Photos: Gary Braasch)

birds were killed by the oil and more than 1,000 sea otters perished. I saw bald eagles with brown oil stains on their white feathers, and workers found at least 150 eagles dead in the mess.

If there was any good to come out the wreck of the *Exxon Valdez*, it was the fact that when the tanker's cargo fouled 1,100 miles of pristine Alaska shoreline, any hope that oilmen held of early access to the Arctic National Wildlife Refuge was scuttled. Even as the huge ship ground her way onto the jagged reef, the industry was gearing up to move exploratory drilling rigs onto the coastal plain because they apparently had the votes in Congress to allow oil development in the refuge. But reports of oil damage and wildlife losses coming out of Prince William Sound were sobering. Senator J. Bennett Johnston of Louisiana, whose committee planned to bring the matter to the Senate floor for a vote, backed off, sensing that the issue would fail in the oily wake of the wrecked tanker.

A decade later, an impatient oil industry still knocks at the refuge gate while conservationists continue to question the nation's need for the oil—if indeed it is there beneath the tundra—and argue that America's only section of protected Arctic coast deserves wilderness designation.

Meanwhile, Dave Cline was also working with native communities to rebuild populations of wild geese on the Yukon-Kuskowim Delta. He was busy nurturing a new partnership between the United States and Russia in the Beringia area which the two countries share. He contested proposals to create new open-pit mines and to build roads through wilderness areas. He also opposed laws that made it easy to hunt down wolves from aircraft.

Dave joined the unending fight against destructive timbering of the Tongass National Forest, largest of all our 153 national forests. This temperate rain forest sprawls over 80 percent of southeast Alaska, covering 16.8 million acres and harboring stands of age-old spruce and hemlock. This is a region of hundreds of islands, coves, and fjords set against backdrops of snow-capped peaks. Its streams run heavy with spawning salmon that feed the eagles and brown bears, and the world's greatest concentration of nesting bald eagles can be found along these waterways. On some shorelines, sky-high eagle nests decorate the tops of towering spruce and hemlocks every mile or so.

Pages 194-195: The immense leaves of skunk cabbage line a rushing stream in southeast Alaska's Misty Fjords National Monument, which is administered by the U.S. Forest Service. (Photo: Carr Clifton/Minden Pictures)

It was low tide and John set his plane down smoothly on the edge of a bay to get a closer look at a female bear and her three cubs feeding near the edge of the woods. We left the plane and slipped quietly into a line of trees to stand in the shadows and watch the family harvesting sedges. Another bear came from the forest and spotted the female. On rare occasions I had seen a lone grizzly or brown bear; now I had five of them in my binoculars at one time. The single bear, unwilling to mix it up with the mother, soon departed. In John's view, we had modest success spotting bears. He recalled one evening census when biologists counted more than 200 bears on Admiralty. The island's total population is estimated at 1,500, one brown bear per square mile, the most concentrated population in the world. John calls this island of salmon and solitude "the best of all worlds for bears."

Aloft again, we flew over other parts of Admiralty Island while John pointed to ancient trails worn six inches deep or more by generations of brown bears that stepped in their ancestor's footprints, following paths that were perhaps thousands of years old over the slopes and along the beaches. Then, passing over nearby Baranof and Chichagof Islands, we saw not bear trails but naked clearcuts left by the timber companies. "If they're going to harvest timber here," John said, "I would prefer to see them designate certain drainages for timber farms and stay out of the rest—leave it for the wildlife."

He is quiet for a moment. "Southeast Alaska," he says, "is a very special place."

Whoops! A spawning sockeye salmon leaps right into the maw of an Alaskan brown bear. (Photo: Thomas D. Mangelsen)

Roger Tory Peterson's first real job was as a schoolteacher, and although he soon abandoned the classroom, he never stopped teaching. He displayed many talents over the years—as a painter, photographer, writer, lecturer, explorer, and expert naturalist—but when asked to define himself, he said he was an educator.

When young Roger was learning to identify birds, the guidebooks were either weighty tomes that gave far too much information or breezy booklets that gave too little. Peterson imagined something in between: a compact book that presented only the key field marks of each species depicted in diagrammatic drawings. Publishers were wary of this approach, but finally, in 1934, Houghton Mifflin cautiously printed 2,000 copies. The print run sold out in two weeks. In the sixty-four years since, Peterson's *Field Guide to the Birds* has never been out of print.

Simplicity was the key to Peterson's system. He believed that recognition of species should not be the realm of just the scientist or the specialist. The nascent hobby of bird watching gained a tremendous boost from Peterson's guide as tens of thousands of readers discovered that they could name the birds they saw.

After the success of his first field guide, Peterson became the education director for the National Audubon Society and the art editor for *Audubon* magazine. Later, he was the art director for the National Wildlife Federation, then struck out on his own. As a freelancer, he wrote or co-wrote five more field guides and numerous other books and articles, created hundreds of paintings, and photographed and filmed birds all over the world. His first bird guide eventually sold several million copies and became the model for a series of more than forty other guidebooks that covered everything from beetles to weather. The Peterson field guides (along with the many imitators that followed) have been credited with helping create the climate of nature appreciation that sparked the environmental movement.

Throughout his career, and through the many honors he received, Peterson remained a modest, gentle individual with a passion for nature. He seemed to gain his greatest satisfaction from inspiring beginners to take notice of the natural world.

—KENN KAUFMAN

Roger Tory Peterson, his wife Virginia, and admirers on Hawk Mountain's North Lookout. (Photo: Hawk Mountain Sanctuary Archives)

1990

The Owl and the Forest

1990 The Owl and the Forest

by Jon R. Luoma

ERIC FORSMAN, AN UNDERGRADUATE STUDENT at Oregon State University, had managed to land a prime job for the summer of 1968: He was hired by the U.S. Forest Service as a fire lookout in the Willamette National Forest, a spectacularly beautiful expanse of conifer forest in the Cascade Mountains. Little did he realize that a few moments of interacting with birds one surprising day would lead him—and the species in question—into a storm of scientific, social, and political turmoil that would not peak until a United States president intervened a quarter-century later. All this young outdoorsman knew was that he was hearing strange, hacking hoots from somewhere in the canopy of the ancient forest surrounding his lookout site.

Mystified, Forsman hooted-barked back, trying to imitate the sound. It worked, for the birds returned the favor and man and forest denizens called back and forth until a pair of mid-sized owls suddenly appeared. They were striking birds with mottled breasts, but for all their apparent boldness, they were creatures that Forsman had never seen before.

In fact, few people had seen northern spotted owls in recent decades, because they are unique to mature forests and, particularly, to the interior depths of towering old-growth forests in the Pacific Northwest. And it was the very sort of habitat that was disappearing quickly from the region.

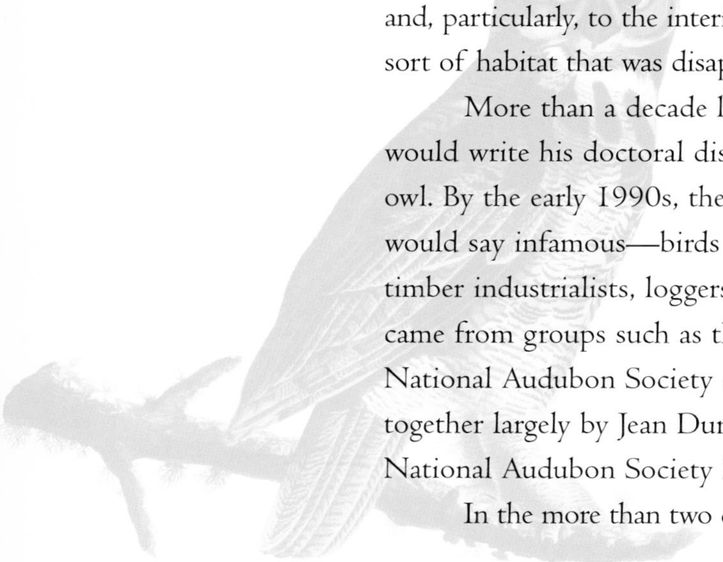

More than a decade later, after a stint in the Army and years of graduate study in wildlife biology, Forsman would write his doctoral dissertation about, and promptly become the world's leading authority on, the spotted owl. By the early 1990s, the owl would be forced out of obscurity to become one of the most famous—some would say infamous—birds in the United States. The species was at the center of a raging conflict that pitted timber industrialists, loggers, and their supporters against concerned scientists and environmentalists. The latter came from groups such as the Oregon Natural Resources Council (a coalition of grassroots groups including six National Audubon Society chapters in the region) and the Ancient Forest Alliance (a national coalition pulled together largely by Jean Durning, the Northwest representative for the Wilderness Society, and Brock Evans, a National Audubon Society lobbyist and passionate proponent of protecting old-growth forests).

In the more than two decades that intervened between Forsman's first interaction with the spotted owl and the

Mist bathes a remnant stand of old-growth Douglas firs in Oregon. "Biodiversity" became a buzzword among conservationists in the late 1980s as biologists began to untangle the web of life in the Northwest's ancient forests. They found, for example, that an imperiled seabird, the marbled murrelet, nests high in these towering coastal trees instead of on the sheer cliffs or grassy islands where most oceanic birds breed. (Photo: Gary Braasch)

dawn of the 1990s, his own research as well as work by other biologists had made it clear that the species was likely doomed to extinction if a trend that had prevailed for most of the century in northern California, Oregon, and Washington continued. The spotted owl is profoundly dependent on ancient forests for nesting and foraging habitat. But in the early 1900s, loggers began leveling the Northwest's diverse stands of Sitka spruce, Douglas fir, and western red cedar. Throughout the region, giant trees came thundering to earth, to be sawed into two-by-fours, shaved into plywood veneers, or ground into paper pulp. In 1983, a group of scientists working out of the Forest Service's Andrews Experiment Forest in Oregon announced that if present trends continued, the only remaining old-growth would be found in national parks, wilderness areas, and other preserves. Those existing reserves, they wrote, "occupy less than 5 percent of the original landscape, and the end of the unreserved old-growth is in sight."

Pages 200-201: *The Hoh Valley rainforest along the Pacific Coast in Olympic National Park protects one of the last stands of great trees on Washington's heavily logged Olympic Peninsula. Long-lived Sitka spruce and Douglas firs —soaring to heights of 200 to 300 feet—lord over this mossy wonderland, thriving on the moderate climate and consistent moisture from rain and fog. (Photo: John Shaw)*

Page 203: *The uncertain fate of the spotted owl was the catalyst for a rancorous and ongoing national debate over management of public and private timberlands in the West. But the docile, vole-eating owl is not the only species threatened by clearcutting. Biologists say that a hundred or more kinds of mammals, birds, amphibians, plants, and insects, as well as the Northwest's fabled salmon runs, are dependent on protection of the remaining old-growth forests. (Photo: Thomas D. Mangelsen)*

Right: *A clearcut block of industrial forestland in Washington. Some scientists say that old-growth can be harvested in a more benign, ecological way if loggers leave ancient trees and logs behind to seed a new forest. But the concept has been greeted with skepticism on both sides of the issue. (Photo: Gary Braasch)*

The best evidence suggested that, for the spotted owl, the fragmented bits and pieces of ancient woods in parks and other preserves would not be enough. In 1985, University of Chicago biologist, Russell Lande, projected that the spotted owl population, already in sharp decline, would almost certainly plummet over the precipice of extinction if the Forest Service continued to allow old-growth to be heavily logged.

In fact, ever since Congress passed the Endangered Species Act in 1973, the spotted owl had been on a list of candidates for designating as imperiled. But remarkably, even after the Lande report, the U.S. Fish and Wildlife Service, under intense pressure from the timber industry and Pacific Northwest politicians, decided not to list the species.

The U.S. Forest Service, meanwhile, attempted to appease timber interests by designing logging schemes that supposedly focused on protecting old-growth reserves but actually set aside blocks of forest that were too small, in many cases, to support the birds. Most notably, the Forest Service recommended habitat protection areas of about 2,200 acres for the owls when research suggested that the birds would need nearly double that amount of space, at least in the northern part of their range in Washington. In 1987, the National Audubon Society released the report of a high-level scientific advisory committee that called for much larger reserves in general, and at least 4,500 acre-reserves in Washington. The panel pointed to the extinction of the ivory-billed woodpecker in the South

Left: *A worker bucks logs in an old-growth clearcut on the Olympic Peninsula. Blame has been heaped on the spotted owl for economic problems in Pacific Northwest timber towns, while mill modernization and the export of unprocessed logs to the Pacific Rim are the real cause of job losses. (Photo: Natalie B. Fobes)*

after most of its old-growth habitat had been cleared, noting that the woodpecker and other species had slipped into extinction due purely to human ignorance. In this case, the panel noted, the owl could vanish as a result of "a considered judgement of a federal agency."

In 1988, after environmentalists sued the Fish and Wildlife Service, a federal court in Seattle harshly ordered the agency to revisit the decision, suggesting it had been both "arbitrary and capricious" in its finding. In March 1989, the court ordered that logging stop on federal lands in spotted owl habitat until the government could prove that clear-cutting had not violated laws regarding the protection of an at-risk species. However, congressmen allied with the timber industry quickly overturned the decision by legislative fiat, attaching to an unrelated bill a rider temporarily enabling massive timber sales on public lands. (The provision would become known among environmentalists as the "Rider from Hell.")

Still, in June 1990, U.S. Fish and Wildlife Service director, John R. Turner, concurred that, "The biological evidence says that the northern spotted owl is in trouble." He declared, "We will not, and by law cannot, ignore that evidence." And Turner at last announced that the spotted owl must indeed be listed as a threatened species. By May 1991, with the Rider from Hell expired, the Seattle court issued another injunction prohibiting logging in spotted-owl country until the government adopted a scientifically sound plan to protect the bird.

In the national news media, the conflict was typically portrayed as one of "owls versus jobs." Never mind that jobs had begun vanishing in droves in the timber-dependent region long before any efforts to protect the spotted owl. A May 1989 industry report noted that in the eight years before 1987, 26,000 jobs had been lost to mechanization in mills even though lumber production had increased by nearly 15 percent. Still, the anger and fear in logging communities was palpable. Bumper stickers read, "Shoot an owl, save a logger," and "I love spotted owls—fried." In the timber town of Forks on the Olympic Peninsula, residents erected a giant cross before a mounded mock grave. On the arms of the cross perched a group of impudent, home-made spotted owls, in effigy, and a large sign read, "Here lie the hopes and dreams of our children." In Oregon, arsonists torched 9,000 acres of old growth that lay within a designed spotted owl reserve. But evidence also abounded that loggers and their communities were being used by an industry bent on ravaging the remaining ancient forests as quickly as possible.

John G. Mitchell, then an *Audubon* field editor, wrote in 1991 of the "acrid stink of manipulation," with a leading industry trade group "purporting to care about jobs in the boondocks when its real mission is to protect profits in the boardrooms of the timber corporations that hide beneath its skirts." But Mitchell was nearly as hard on the national environmental groups, suggesting that they had "cruelly ignored—written off" the people of the timber towns.

Meanwhile, the first of what would be a series of more detailed reports on the spotted owl's habitat

Activists demonstrate in the rain outside a "Forest Summit" called by newly elected President Bill Clinton, who hoped to find a compromise acceptable to all sides in the old-growth dispute. Some environmentalists have since called for a complete ban on all logging in the national forests. (Photo: Gary Braasch)

needs was released in 1990 by a government-sponsored team of scientists led by wildlife biologist, Jack Ward Thomas. For the timber industry, that report, which focused only on the needs of the owl, came as a shock: The scientists suggested that protecting the owl would demand a 25-percent reduction of timber output on national forest lands in the region.

Two years later, during the 1992 presidential campaign, little had been resolved. The court injunction remained in place, and the conflict was still raging. But Democratic candidate, Bill Clinton, carried the region, almost certainly because he promised to sit down with all sides of the debate and find a suitable compromise. Indeed, Clinton in the first weeks of his presidency staged a showy summit between key players in the dispute—scientists, environmentalists, loggers, and timber industry officials—and his own highest ranking aides and advisors, including Vice President Al Gore and Interior Secretary Bruce Babbit. The conference was a sort of policy-wonk happening in which the new president allowed all sides to pitch their point of view. In its wake, Thomas, who would soon become the first scientist-chief of the U.S. Forest Service, agreed to head another scientific panel—the fourth in as many years—to look at the owl in particular and the ancient forest ecosystem in general.

In many ways, a changing perspective in spotted-owl country reflected what had become a rapid shift in perspective among both biologists and environmentalists. Concerns about the survival of individual species had begun to broaden in the 1980s to concerns about entire complexes of species and the ecosystems they depended on. It had become clear that, in many places, a full range of "biodiversity" was at risk. Since the first spotted owl panel had completed its work, new information had emerged about other species that are dependent on old growth, or benefit by sharp restrictions on logging. An alarming report commissioned by the Portland Audubon Society in 1988 revealed that an imperiled seabird, the marbled murrelet, also depended profoundly on old-growth trees as nesting sites. By 1993, scientists would conclude that more than 100 species of mammals, birds, amphibians, plants, and insects were dependent on old growth

***Pages 208-209:** A bull elk, its antlers still sheathed in velvet, surveys a misty mountain meadow. A subspecies called the Roosevelt elk inhabits rainforest along the Northwest coast and has shorter but heavier antlers than its Rocky Mountain relatives. (Photo: Daniel J. Cox/ Natural Exposures)*

for survival, ranging from the tiny, mouselike red-backed vole to the Pacific giant salamander to the Vaux's swift to the Roosevelt elk.

Of particular concern in the Northwest was the region's fantastically rich but declining stock of salmon. Salmon depend on the protection that forests offer to streams in a multitude of ways, including the cooling shade of boughs over small headwater streams and streamside erosion control that intact roots systems provide.

Initially the Thomas committee came up with eight options for President Clinton to consider. Even the most pro-timber plan called for a reduction of logging to about 700 million board feet of timber per year, down from a peak of more than 3 billion board feet in the 1980s. (A board foot measures one foot by one foot by one inch.) The most restrictive option would have nearly eliminated logging altogether. But committee leader, Thomas, convinced that such sharp reductions would be politically impossible, came up with a ninth option that would release as much as 1.2 billion board feet for removal through an elaborate scheme that allowed some "salvage" logging of dead and dying timber in old growth reserves and selective removal of some younger trees as well. The plan called for wide forested corridors around streams that would connect with large blocks of old-growth in an attempt to partially mimic the layout of truly wild land. To help boost the log output, the plan placed about one-fourth of the region's old growth in large (80,000- to 100,000-acre) "adaptive management areas," where foresters could experiment with various schemes aimed at protecting more native biodiversity than would be possible with traditional clearcutting.

A green head and bright-red body identify a spawning sockeye salmon. Several kinds of Pacific Northwest salmon have been declared threatened under the federal Endangered Species Act, in part because of damage to spawning streams from clearcuts. (Photo: Natalie B. Fobes)

For instance, forest ecologist, Jerry F. Franklin, who had served on the committee, championed an approach he called "New Forestry" in which logging schemes would attempt to emulate nature's own patterns of disturbance. Franklin and a group of colleagues had noted that forest stands in the fire-prone Northwest appear to be well adapted to recover after fire, but that even the most intense fires do not devastate a landscape as thoroughly as wholesale clearcutting. Old growth can be harvested in a more ecologically sound way, he and his supporters contend, if loggers leave some ancient trees standing along with giant logs on the forest floor. This approach, they argue, will lead to a more structurally and biologically diverse ecosystem as new trees grow up.

But although such "ecosystem management" approaches have generated some enthusiasm among government foresters and even one major timber company in the region, many on all sides of the old-growth debate remain deeply skeptical. On the one hand, New Forestry requires loggers to "waste," as they see it, valuable timber by leaving trees and logs behind. On the other, a site logged in such a fashion is at least as ugly as a clearcut, and perhaps worse, since the scattering of forest giants left behind serves as a bitter reminder of a cathedral-like woods that has been felled.

At the end of the 1990s, the door has not yet closed on the old-growth debate. Logging interests continue to decry the dramatic drop in timber output in the region. Some environmentalists, meanwhile, called for a "zero cut" ban on logging in national forests, not just in the Pacific Northwest but nationwide. Meanwhile, future forest battles loom large. The primeval pine forests of the Great Lake states were

Mount Ranier rises over a reforested clearcut in Washington's North Cascades. Biologically rich old-growth forests typically are replaced with monoculture tree farms which will be cut again as soon as the trunks are large enough for the mill. (Photo: Natalie B. Fobes)

Pages 212-213: *A misty autumn morning in Great Smoky Mountains National Park. Not far away, on and around Tennessee's Cumberland Plateau, gigantic chip mills are chewing up forests that boast a mixture of hardwood trees found nowhere else in America. The chips are shipped to paper pulp mills as far away as Japan. (Photo: David Muench)*

leveled just before and just after the turn of the twentieth century. Millions of acres of these cutover lands have since recovered dramatically. But some parts of the region—notably in northern Minnesota—are being logged more heavily than any other national forest lands, and projections suggest that lumber and pulpwood production will continue to soar in the early years of the twenty-first century. The region, which includes not only the five Great Lakes but thousands of smaller inland lakes and thousands of miles of streams, is one of the nation's most prized areas for vacation homes and outdoor recreation. And although protests over logging in the region have generally been muted, conflict seems inevitable.

The pinelands of the South have long been prized and productive timberlands. Humid, with mild winters, the region grows trees rapidly. But grassroots environmentalists and the National Audubon Society have expressed alarm over what some of the industry's own consultants say is an unsustainable rate of logging. Of particular concern in the South is the new logging in a unique region called the mixed mesophytic forest on and around Tennessee's Cumberland Plateau. One of the most spectacular and rare ecosystems on the planet, the mixed mesophytic forest is characterized by a dramatic diversity of hardwood tree species. In fact, the only comparable woodlands lie in central China. In the late 1990s, environmentalists and wildlife biologists in the region began to express alarm about the sudden arrival of gigantic "chip-mills" that grind up whole trees into tiny chips about the size of a small snack-cracker. The chips are shipped to mills—some in the region, some as far away as Japan—to be further ground into high quality paper pulp. Despite conclusive evidence that clear-cutting in such hardwood forests can cause permanent damage, it is the method of choice for most logging operations feeding the chip mills.

In general, proponents of conventional forestry

point out that trees can be, and typically are, replaced by seedlings and in time a new forest will grow on a site. Environmentalists counter that, all too often, replanting schemes mean that a wild and diverse woodland is replaced by a monoculture of whichever species happens to be most desired by the timber industry. For instance, throughout the Pacific Northwest replanted Douglas firs, prized for their fine, sturdy wood, grow like rows of giant cornstalks; in much of the Great Lakes region similar croplike rows of red pine or sweeping stands of aspen grow.

Even in the mixed mesophytic forest, chipmill operators acknowledge that they have little interest in promoting a truly natural and diverse forest. In fact, they intend to eliminate outright from their lands some key species, notably hickories, which have a tenacious bark that is all but impossible to remove at mills. Biologists are worried that widespread clearcutting, and a move away from forest diversity, might lead to dramatic reductions in food for wildlife, even if new trees grow in the place of older forests. Many species, ranging from deer to bears to foxes and squirrels, feed on "hard mast" like hickory nuts and acorns from oaks.

"Many of the oak species don't even start to produce a good output of acorns until they're thirty, forty, fifty years old," says U.S. Fish and Wildlife Service biologist, Lee Barklay. Yet industry plans to clear cut sites as rapidly as every three decades to feed the region's chip-mills. Continues Barklay, "That means that they're going to be cutting trees again just as they're reaching the point where they're beginning to produce the mast that wildlife need."

The National Audubon Society recently initiated a Forest Habit Campaign aimed at coordinating science with national and grassroots advocacy to sustain and restore America's forest ecosystems.

Meanwhile, another key issue that crystallized

A white-tailed deer licks a sugar maple's sweet spring sap. Biologists warn that widespread clearcutting of the East's old hardwood forests to feed chip mills will harm an array of wild animals, including deer, black bears, and squirrels, that depend on the mast crops of oaks and hickories. (Daniel J. Cox/Natural Exposures)

Just a five-hour drive from New York City and Boston lies a state-run park that is bigger than Yellowstone, Yosemite, Grand Canyon, Glacier, and Olympic national parks combined. In fact, at 6 million acres, the Adirondack Park is larger than Massachusetts.

Within the park, established by New York State in 1892, there are more than 3,000 lakes and ponds, 30,000 miles of running water, and 2,000 peaks that by local standards qualify as mountains. But above all, the Adirondacks are a place of trees: 200,000 acres of virgin forest and more than a million acres of decades-old second growth.

One of the more unusual aspects of the park is that ordinary citizens can own property and live full-time within its borders. Less than half the park actually belongs to New York. And although those 2.7 million acres, known as the forest preserve, constitute the best-protected wildlands in the country, the rest of the park is private property. The vast majority of it is to some degree either developed or vulnerable to development.

The dynamic between public and private shaped the park's past and continues to drive its future. In the 1890s urban sportsmen who were concerned about losing their playground to logging joined industrialists, seeking to protect the water that filled their canals. Together they pushed to create a public forest preserve. Since then, grassroots conservationists have fought with varying degrees of success against efforts to dam rivers, to fill the park with hotels, and to develop private land.

Recently the goal has shifted back to expansion: Last June New York spent $17.1 million to buy nearly 15,000 acres from the estate of industrialist William C. Whitney. But it is not clear whether the state will buy or negotiate easements for the more than 500,000 acres that are currently for sale in the Adirondacks. And so America's largest experiment in sustainable development continues. The Adirondacks are both one of the nation's most stunning conservation successes and one of the greatest challenges for future generations.

—Paul Schneider

New York's Adirondack Park is famous for its postcard views. (Photo: Carr Clifton/Minden Pictures)

in the 1990s is intimately linked to the forests of the Appalachian region. All along the spine of that mountain chain, red spruce trees have been in decline. Studies have confirmed that the problem is linked directly to pollution that regularly bathes Appalachian mountaintops, including both ozone-laden smog that drifts from cities and industrial centers as well as a potent pollutant virtually no one had heard of when the first Clean Air Act was passed: acid rain.

Precipitation—rain, snow, fog—can become

Left: *Acid fog that envelopes the Appalachian ridgeline is blamed for the decline of red spruce stands in the Great Smoky Mountains. (Photo: Jenny Hager/The Image Works)*

Opposite: *Geologically sensitive areas like Adirondack Park in northern New York, where there is little acid-buffering limestone in the soil, are hard hit by acid fallout. This stream flows from one of more than 200 Adirondack lakes that have been acidified, eliminating fish populations and other aquatic life. (Photo: Carr Clifton/Minden Pictures)*

acidic when the gases sulfur dioxide and nitrogen oxide react with water in the atmosphere. The pollutants come from sources as diverse as coal-fired powerplants, refineries, and automobiles. The acid-rain issue rose to national prominence early in the 1980s, and for the entire decade a debate raged between environmentalists and industrial polluters about the seriousness of the problem. By the dawn of the 1990s, a consensus had emerged among scientists. It had become clear that acid rain could destroy fish and other living things in lakes and rivers.

The good news was that acid rain harms only aquatic ecosystems in regions that are geologically sensitive. The bad news was that those vulnerable regions, where rocks and soil contain minimal amounts of limestone or similar acid-buffering compounds, often are some of the most prized natural areas in the United States. These areas include the lake-dotted Adirondack Park in northern New York (where more than 200 lakes had been acidified by the early 1980s), much of northern New England, and the spectacular lakeland wilderness called the Boundary Waters Canoe Area in northern Minnesota. Even more striking, much of eastern Canada lies on a vast shield of granite with little capacity to buffer acid, and includes literally hundreds of thousands of vulnerable lakes, some 14,000 of which have already been acidified to the point where fish populations have been eliminated.

By 1990, research showed that some sensitive lakes in both the U.S. and Canada (as well as in Scandinavia) were ten to one hundred times more acidic than they had been in preindustrial times. At least as worrisome, scientists documented that acid rain caused dramatic changes in soils, leaching out calcium and magnesium, both important nutrients for plant growth. Acid rain was causing about $2 billion in damage to the man-made environment (buildings, monuments, cars) just in the eastern U.S. And there

Page 218: *Wildfire is a natural part of the forest regime in the Northwest, but even the most intense fires will not devastate the landscape as thoroughly as clearcutting. (Fritz Hoffman/The Image Works)*

Pages 218–219: *Redwoods and rhododendrons in Del Norte State Park, one of three primeval forest areas that were bought early in the century by the Save the-Redwoods League and now form the core of Redwood National Park. (Photo: Darrell Gulin)*

was broad agreement that red spruce and perhaps other trees ranging from Frasier fir to sugar maple were being harmed.

In a major victory for environmentalists, Congress revised the Clean Air Act in 1990 (the original version was passed in 1970), including stringent controls on the main pollutant that causes acid rain. Overall, the law requires a halving of sulfur dioxide emissions from 20 million tons per year in 1990 to 10 million tons by 2010. But even as the revised Clean Air Act was bringing a degree of resolution to the acid-rain problem, a new atmospheric scourge, global warming, was looming as a more daunting problem. Like acid rain, global warming is closely linked to burning fossil fuels. But unlike any conventional pollution problem, it cannot be solved simply by filtering away a polluting gas or solid.

The primary cause of global warming is an excess of carbon dioxide in the atmosphere, and carbon dioxide is an unavoidable byproduct of fuel combustion. Simply put, as the world has industrialized, as cars and air conditioners and a host of modern conveniences have proliferated, energy consumption has soared. High in the atmosphere, carbon dioxide and other gases naturally help trap heat, a "greenhouse effect" that makes Earth's climate hospitable for life. But since the dawn of the Industrial Revolution, concentrations of carbon dioxide in the atmosphere have risen about 30 percent. Most scientists who have studied the issue believe that continuing increases will lead inevitably to a warmer world.

Trees—"the lungs of the planet" in the words of Franklin Roosevelt—use enormous quantities of carbon dioxide. But widespread deforestation is aggravating the problem, particularly in the tropics where forests are often cleared with fire for farming. In fact, the climate has already warmed roughly one degree Fahrenheit in this century, and the U.S. Environmental Protection Agency has projected that if present trends continue, the average temperature of our planet could increase by as much as five degrees in the next 100 years.

A warming planet means a rising sea level as glaciers and polar ice caps melt and expand, a clear threat to low-lying coastal regions and islands. Computer models suggest that hurricanes and other storms would be more frequent and more fierce in a warmer world, while some rich crop-growing regions could be stricken with drought. A rapidly warming planet could destroy habitat for a wide range of wildlife and plant species, particularly in marginally protected ecosystems.

At the end of the twentieth century, some hope for global action on global warming is materializing. Late in 1997, in Kyoto, Japan, the world's industrial nations agreed to a protocol that would reduce carbon dioxide and other greenhouse gas emissions below 1990 levels, starting in 2008. However, political resistance to the treaty remained intense, especially in the

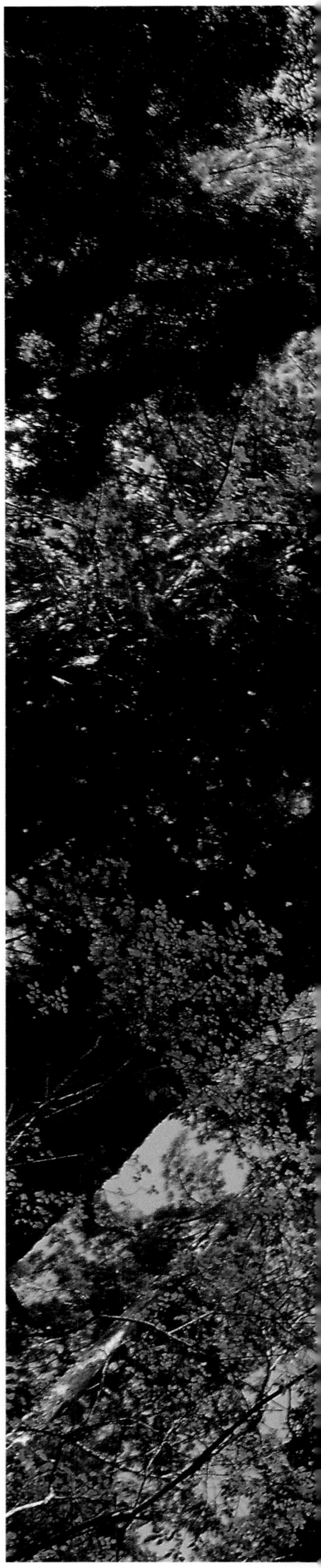

U.S., the world's largest emitter of greenhouse gases. American industry and union lobbyists fear that the situation could lead to sharp reductions in manufacturing and jobs, particularly since developing nations were not subject to mandatory reductions. Although a small handful of developing nations, led by Argentina, have since agreed to voluntary reductions, other key countries including both China and India have not, and the treaty's real impact on global warming remains uncertain.

In the face of a panoply of environmental problems that sometimes seems overwhelming, it might be worthwhile to gain some perspective from the past 100 years of conservation history. Perhaps the most dramatic single aspect is the shift in human consciousness about nature and our role in it, especially

After fire burned 10,000 acres of Maine's Acadia National Park in 1947, the original spruce-fir forest was replaced with sun-loving deciduous trees including red maples. (Photo: Carr Clifton/ Minden Pictures)

Oceans are home to animals of unimagined beauty and grace. This primordial vessel of life covers three-quarters of our planet's surface. Yet, as land-bound creatures, we humans have been slow to realize that marine ecosystems and wildlife, just like their terrestrial counterparts, need to be safeguarded.

Until recently, we have thought of fish only as food and commodity, forgetting—or not considering—that fish are wildlife, too. The mission of the National Audubon Society is to conserve and restore natural ecosystems, focusing on birds, other wildlife, and their habitats for the benefit of humanity and the Earth's biological diversity. As the marine conservation program of Audubon, Living Oceans' mission is to reverse the mismanagement of fisheries (nationally and internationally) which has led to the depletion of marine wildlife, and to restore the health of our marine environment and coastal habitats...because fish are wildlife, too.

Living Oceans' staff analyze technical scientific information and translate these into non-technical terms and principles for policy makers, develop new fishery management policies based on their scientific analyses, and influence the reform of existing national and international policies to optimize the economic and ecological sustainability of living marine resources. Living Oceans' staff participate in several inter-organizational partnerships, serving as conduits of information between international scientific and management bodies and conservationists as they collectively develop policy strategies. Living Oceans' membership consists of Audubon chapter members and many concerned citizens outside the Audubon family. With the information provided to them by the program, they have become active constituents on behalf of marine conservation.

The marine conservation staff educates the public through public speaking ventures, collaborations with aquariums, a quarterly publication, *Living Oceans News*, media outreach, educational curricula, and written articles.

—Carl Safina and Mercédès Lee

in the last two or three decades. It would be unthinkable today for a government agency to set out to eliminate a native predator from the national parks, or for a politician from any party to propose a return to free-for-all air and water pollution or the kind of cut-and-run (and erode-and-ruin) logging that prevailed at the turn of the century. Poll after poll has shown that Americans in the last years of the century are conservationists by nature. And through the murk and gloom of today's problems, it surely is worth considering progress made: the dramatic expansion of refuge and wilderness lands; the resurrection of Lake Erie; and the return to biological vigor of populations of once-imperiled species such as the peregrine falcon, a bird that had seemed doomed thirty years ago. The peregrine's recent removal from North America's list of imperiled wildlife proved, said National Audubon Society spokesman, Daniel P. Beard, that "the Endangered Species Act is working."

We do face daunting problems, but also the hope of solving them if only we can choose the path that, as Rachael Carson described it, will provide "our last, our only chance to reach a destination that assures the preservation of our earth."

Chronology:
100 Years of Conservation–1899 to 1999

by Frank Graham Jr.

THE STAGE WAS SET IN 1899 for a great leap forward by the young bird protection movement. George Bird Grinnell, a prominent sportsman and editor, had founded the first Audubon Society thirteen years earlier to counter the unrestricted slaughter of wild birds for plumes, flesh, and fun. Chief among the threats were gunners hired by the millinery industry to provide the feathers then in great demand for women's hats and gowns. Then, in 1887, Grinnell issued a publication of news and exhortation called *Audubon Magazine.*

Both the society and the publication quickly expired. But the idea lived on. In 1896 a group of society women and concerned sportsmen in the Boston area appropriated the name of the great painter of birds, John James Audubon, to launch their own campaign against the ongoing slaughter. They called their organization the Massachusetts Audubon Society. Lovers of birds in other states signed on, founding their own societies to educate the public and lobby their legislators.

Enter a new magazine, dedicated to wild birds and their protection.

DECADE 1899–1909

1899

The bimonthly magazine *Bird-Lore* makes its first appearance in February. Launched by Frank M. Chapman, the American Museum of Natural History's celebrated ornithologist, it devotes a section to news from the scattered state Audubon Societies and draws the new movement together. Forty years later, the magazine changes its name to *Audubon.*

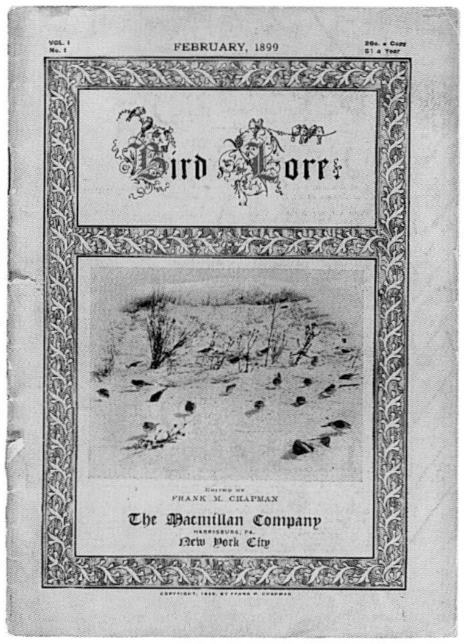

The first issue of Bird-Lore *is published by The Macmillan Company in February of 1899. (Photo courtesy* Audubon *magazine)*

1900

Congress passes the Lacey Act, banning the shipment from one state to another of birds killed in violation of state laws. This gives the new bird protection movement its first effective weapon against the plume and market hunters. In December, *Bird-Lore* proposes a positive alternative—a Christmas Bird Count to replace the traditional shooting competitions on that holiday.

1901

Theodore Roosevelt becomes president of the United States after the assassination of William McKinley. The new president's early association with the Audubon Society of the District of Columbia puts him in tune with the movement, which now has 36 state societies. Gifford Pinchot, the nation's chief forester, gains enormous influence as Roosevelt's adviser on natural resources.

1902

Congress passes the Reclamation Act, which helps revolutionize land use in the West by funding massive irrigation projects and establishing the precursor of the Bureau of Reclamation. Back East, the American Ornithologists' Union hires a warden, Guy Bradley, to protect wading bird colonies in Florida from plume hunters.

1903

Roosevelt creates the first federal wildlife refuge on Florida's Pelican Island. As the refuge originates by executive order, it receives no funds from Congress and warden Paul Kroegel is paid $7 a month by the Audubon Societies.

1904

During November a wealthy businessman, Albert Wilcox, approaches Audubon leaders with a proposal to incorporate the various state societies into a national organization. The lure is a legacy of $100,000, which Wilcox agrees to leave to the new organization, along with funds for an office and a part-time secretary. Within days, a lawyer draws up papers of incorporation.

1905

On January 30 the National Association of Audubon Societies for the Protection of Wild Birds and Animals is incorporated in New York State. William Dutcher, insurance company executive and prominent amateur ornithologist, becomes its first president. The state societies remain as independent organizations within the new federation. Six months later Guy Bradley, by then an Audubon warden, is murdered by a poacher at the southern tip of Florida.

Guy Bradley is hired as the first Audubon game warden in 1902. (Photo courtesy the National Audubon Society)

Mule deer moving at dusk, Yosemite National Park in California. (Photo: Galen Rowell)

Colonel Theodore Roosevelt investigating a sea-swept colony of royal terns on Grand Cochese Island, Louisiana, in June 1915. (Photo courtesy the National Audubon Society)

Least tern chick on Gilgo Beach, Long Island, New York. (Photo: Arthur Morris/Birds As Art)

1906

After a long fight by Sierra Club founder John Muir, Congress votes to incorporate a neglected California state park, Yosemite, into the federal government and designates it a national park.

1907

After Roosevelt creates the Inland Waterways Commission to come up with a comprehensive plan for their development, Congress balks at surrendering its haphazard logrolling schemes and rejects the commission's proposals.

1908

Poachers murder two more Audubon wardens, Columbus G. MacLeod in Florida and L. P. Reeves in South Carolina. As in the Bradley killing, no one is ever convicted. Congress moves to quash Roosevelt's water and forest protection initiatives, while a split develops between advocates of Gifford Pinchot's utilitarian brand of resource development and John Muir's preservation ideas.

1909

Hearing that an island sheltering an important tern colony in Massachusetts is being considered as the site of a state home for lepers, Audubon president William Dutcher reflects, "It would not be a bad thing for the terns as the lepers would keep people away more effectively than laws or wardens."

DECADE 1910–1919

1910

William Dutcher's final achievement is passage in New York of the Audubon

Plumage Act, banning sale or possession of the feathers of birds in the same family as any species protected in the state. As all native herons, egrets, and terns are already protected there, the bill cripples the plume trade at its very center. When Dutcher suffers a disabling stroke, the board of directors installs his aide, T. Gilbert Pearson, as chief executive officer.

1911

William Hornaday, first director of the Bronx Zoo and most combative conservationist of his day, sparks passage in New York State of the Bayne Act, stopping the sale of native wild game in markets and restaurants. Later that year, California and Massachusetts follow suit.

1912

Theodore Roosevelt, his conservation initiatives undone by the William H. Taft Administration, runs for president as an independent. His exuberant remark, "I am feeling like a bull moose," gives his party a name, but he loses to Woodrow Wilson.

1913

John Muir loses his desperate battle to save his beloved Hetch Hetchy Valley near Yosemite. San Francisco's water advocates move to submerge it beneath a huge reservoir. Hornaday joins with Audubon to have a clause inserted into the Federal Tariff Act, banning the importation to the U.S. of many exotic bird plumes.

1914

Martha, the last passenger pigeon on Earth, dies in the Cincinnati Zoo.

1915

Congress creates Rocky Mountain National Park. A move is made to break the "forever wild" clause in the New York State constitution protecting the Adirondack Park . The attempt to cut "diseased" trees

William Hornaday, first director of the New York Zoological Society (now the Wildlife Conservation Society), helps stop the sale of native game in New York state in 1911. (Photo courtesy the Denver Public Library)

Frank M. Chapman, celebrated ornithologist and founder of Bird-Lore *magazine. (Photo courtesy the American Museum of Natural History)*

Martha, the last passenger pigeon on Earth, at the Cincinnati Zoo. (Photo courtesy the National Audubon Society)

The last captive Carolina parakeet dies in the Cincinnati Zoo in 1918. (Photo: Tom McHugh)

in the park is beaten with the help of an impassioned speech by Louis Marshall, prominent reformer and Zionist, and father of wilderness advocate, Robert Marshall.

1916

Congress approves the creation of the National Park Service, and a wealthy proponent of the system, Stephen T. Mather, is named its chief. The surge of park visitors is directly linked to an increase in cheap automobiles.

1917

The U.S. enters World War I. President Wilson, dramatizing a threatened food shortage, turns out sheep on the White House lawn, while western stockmen and miners try to pry open the national parks under the guise of patriotism—and 5,000 head of cattle get in.

1918

Congress passes an enabling act ratifying the Migratory Bird Treaty Act with Great Britain (representing Canada). The act gives migratory birds protection by the federal government. *Bird-Lore* editor Frank Chapman notes that now the Audubon Association is relieved "of the necessity of watching the legislation of every state and of combating the numberless attempts to legalize the destruction of birds for private gain."

1919

Three-quarters of a million people visit the national parks. Congress creates Lafayette (later Acadia) National Park in Maine, while the National Parks and Conservation Association is formed as an advocate and constructive critic of the Park Service. Huge drainage projects in western wetlands prompt Audubon to join federal wildlife officials in calling for the purchase of prime waterfowl habitat.

DECADE 1920–1929

1920

Congress passes the Mineral Leasing Act, regulating mining on federal lands. William Dutcher dies and T. Gilbert Pearson becomes the official president of the National Association of Audubon Societies.

1921

Aldo Leopold of the U.S. Forest Service formulates a wilderness concept for the national forests. It leads, three years later, to the setting aside of 575 acres for wilderness and recreation in the Gila National Forest in New Mexico, where he works. Planner and forester, Benton MacKaye, promotes the idea of an "Appalachian Trail" through the eastern mountains.

1922

Gilbert Pearson tours Europe. In England, with the help of Lord Edward Grey, he forms the International Committee for Bird Protection and is named its president.

1923

Conservationists help expose the misdeeds of Albert B. Fall, President Warren G. Harding's Interior Secretary. After Congress documents his role in the illegal sale to the Mammoth Oil Company of drilling rights in the nation's oil reserve at Teapot Dome, Wyoming, Fall resigns and eventually goes to prison.

1924

The Audubon Association opens its first sanctuaries: the Rainey Sanctuary in the Louisiana marshes, a gift of Grace Rainey Rogers, and the Theodore Roosevelt Sanctuary on Long Island, New York, given by the Roosevelt family. The Upper Mississippi Wildlife and Fish Refuge is approved by Congress.

T. Gilbert Pearson becomes the second president of the National Association of Audubon Societies in 1920. (Photo courtesy the National Audubon Society)

A flock of snow geese rests during the fall migration. (Photo: Lans Lanting/Minden Pictures)

A swarm of Mexican freetail bats departs Carlsbad Caverns, New Mexico, for a night of feasting on insects. (Photo courtesy the National Park Service)

1925

Aldo Leopold expresses his theory of game management: "We have learned that game is a crop, which Nature will grow, and grow abundantly, provided only we furnish the seed and a suitable environment."

1926

The conservation movement continues to gain public support.

1927

A history of serious floods on the Mississippi River prompts Congress to pass the Rivers and Harbors Act, pushing forward plans concerning navigation, water power, flood control, and irrigation for more than 200 U.S. streams. Meanwhile, federal authorities charge that liquor bootleggers are also bootlegging wild ducks to the market.

1928

Americans buy 6.5 million hunting licenses, adding to pressures on waterfowl already reeling under liberal bag limits and widespread drainage of wetlands.

1929

Audubon's long struggle to preserve waterfowl, drumming up support among its members and professional wildlife managers, culminates in the passage by Congress of the Norbeck-Andersen Act. The legislation makes funds available to federal agencies to buy key wetlands for use as refuges.

DECADE 1930–1939

1930

Congress designates New Mexico's Carlsbad Caverns (home to millions of bats) as a national park. The courts strike down an attempt to build a bobsled run for the 1932 Olympic Games through "forever wild" land in New York's Adirondack Park. The run is finally built on private land at Lake Placid.

1931

Rosalie Edge, a New York reformer and Audubon life member, discovers that Louisiana fur trappers are permitted to take muskrats on the Rainey Sanctuary. Though Gilbert Pearson argues that the rodents are depleting vegetation used by waterfowl, Edge and her supporters force him to back down. From then on Edge leads a bitter attack on Pearson's policies.

1932

Franklin D. Roosevelt is elected to the first of his four terms as U.S. president. Not since his cousin Theodore's administration have conservation issues enjoyed such high priority in the White House. FDR's projects to fight the Great Depression will include the Civilian Conservation Corps, which puts two million unemployed young men to work on forest protection, soil conservation, and other jobs in the national parks and forests.

1933

Despite cries from private power interests that legislation creating the Tennessee Valley Authority is a "socialist idea" and a "Russian bill," FDR signs it into law. The dam and reservoir, built at Muscle Shoals on the Tennessee River, provides the nation's most poverty-stricken major river basin with electric power, flood and erosion control, and diversified industries.

1934

The Audubon Association's membership, decimated by the Depression and Rosalie Edge's vendetta against Pearson, falls from more than 7,000 in the late 1920s to 3,400. Pearson is forced out and John Baker, investment banker and birdwatcher, takes over as executive director.

Joseph Taylor, Roger Tory Peterson, Marion Ingersol, Francis Trembley, Maurice Broun, and Peter and Rosalie Edge at Hawk Mountain Sanctuary, c. 1950. (Photo courtesy Hawk Mountain Sanctuary Archives)

Ernie Johnson, Jesse Allen, Robert Marshall, and Kenneth Harvey in Wiseman, Alaska, prior to Doonerak or Bust trip, 1938. (Photo courtesy The Wilderness Society)

J. N. "Ding" Darling, proponent of the Migratory Bird Hunting Stamp Act and designer of the first federal duck stamp. (Photo courtesy the J. N. "Ding" Darling Foundation)

John Baker with Ray Barnes on Florida Bay, 1941. (Photo courtesy the National Audubon Society)

Publication of Roger Tory Peterson's *Field Guide to the Birds* converts thousands of people to Baker's favorite pastime.

1935

The Audubon Association buys *Bird-Lore* from Frank Chapman. Roger Tory Peterson, Audubon's education director, redesigns the magazine. Kermit Roosevelt, TR's son, is named Audubon president and works closely with executive director Baker. Robert Marshall, with support from Aldo Leopold and Benton MacKaye, organizes The Wilderness Society.

1936

Baker opens the Audubon Nature Camp on Hog Island off the Maine coast, providing conservation education for adults. The National Wildlife Federation is founded at the suggestion of cartoonist and activist J.N. "Ding" Darling.

1937

Congress, with the Pittman-Robertson Act, uses an excise tax on sporting arms and ammunition to fund wildlife restoration projects. Waterfowl enthusiasts form Ducks Unlimited. Ornithologist James Tanner of Cornell receives an Audubon Research Fellowship for a study of the ivory-billed woodpecker, just as the bird is vanishing into extinction.

1938

The Audubon Association buys a building on Fifth Avenue in New York City, opposite the Metropolitan Museum of Art.

1939

A reorganization act in Congress transfers the Agriculture Department's Bureau of the Biological Survey to Interior, creating the new U.S. Fish and Wildlife Service. John Baker funds studies on two more endangered species, the California condor by Carl

Koford and the roseate spoonbill by Robert Porter Allen. The results are published later, along with the ivory-bill study, as the landmark *Audubon Research Reports.*

DECADE 1940–1949

1940

President Roosevelt signs the Bald Eagle Protection Act. On the advice of a consulting firm, John Baker brings the Audubon Association into the modern era: *Bird-Lore*'s name is changed to *Audubon Magazine* (later just plain *Audubon*) and the organization itself becomes the National Audubon Society.

1941

The Japanese bomb Pearl Harbor. The Honolulu Audubon Society cancels its Christmas Bird Count because of travel restrictions in Hawaii. Participants on the San Diego count are stopped five times by military personnel on the lookout for "saboteurs and spies."

1942

An atomic reactor goes into operation at the University of Chicago. Eleanor King becomes editor of *Audubon* and, without John Baker's knowledge, soon finds enough money in the budget to begin paying reasonable fees to well-known writers such as Donald Culross Peattie and Edwin Way Teale.

1943

The Audubon Screen Tours debut this fall in Detroit. A success from the beginning, the program reaches a new audience in dozens of cities throughout the country with its conservation message. Top nature photographers, including Roger Tory Peterson, Olin S. Pettingill, Jr., and Karl Mazlowski, fill an important niche in these pre-TV days.

Carl Koford with a condor chick in Sespe area of Ventura County, California. (Photo: Ed Harrison)

Rachel Carson (with Carl Buchheister) receiving the Audubon Medal at the 1963 Audubon Annual Dinner. (Photo courtesy the National Audubon Society)

Atomic bomb testing at Nevada Proving Grounds, 1951. (Photo: USAF/Science Source)

First issue of Audubon Magazine *after changing its name from* Bird-Lore *in 1940. (Photo courtesy W. Pomeroy)*

1944

Congress creates Big Bend National Park in Texas. John Baker, Audubon's executive director for a decade, is named president by the board of directors and Carl Buchheister becomes his vice-president. Buchheister begins extensive trips to persuade local bird clubs to become Audubon "branches," taking a big step toward the chapter system.

1945

Audubon becomes partners with the Fish and Wildlife Service in the Whooping Crane Project, trying to salvage a species whose population has dwindled to near the vanishing point.

1946

Congress creates the Atomic Energy Commission to guide the awesome new technology toward peacetime uses. The International Whaling Commission is established but is in for rough sailing: General Douglas MacArthur, ruling over U.S.-occupied Japan, jump-starts that war-ravaged country's economy by putting it into the whaling business in a big way.

1947

A long-time Audubon goal is reached with the designation of Everglades National Park. Congress passes the Federal Insecticide, Fungicide, and Rodenticide Act, a flimsy defense against the rising postwar tide of powerful, long-lasting pesticides. The first Audubon Medal is presented to Hugh H. Bennett of the U.S. Soil Conservation Service. *Audubon Field Notes,* the quarterly "birder's bible," appears as a separate publication.

1948

The worst air pollution disaster in U.S. history occurs in Donora, PA, an industrial center where the intense smog is blamed for twenty deaths and at least 5,000 illnesses. After more than 100 failed tries in the past sixty years, Congress finally passes the first Water Pollution Control Act.

1949

A Sand County Almanac, a classic in the literature of nature and conservation written by Aldo Leopold, is published. Olaus Murie, president of The Wilderness Society, eloquently represents his organization and the Sierra Club in a public hearing to help stop a plan to build a dam that threatens Montana's Glacier National Park.

DECADE 1950–1959

1950

Los Angeles begins its long struggle to force the auto industry to install emission-control devices on its products. A Ford spokesman replies assuringly to the city's complaints: "The Ford engineering staff, although mindful that automobile engines produce exhaust gases, feels that these waste vapors are dissipated in the atmosphere quickly and do not present an air pollution problem."

1951

The Nature Conservancy is organized, revolutionizing the efforts of nongovernmental organizations to preserve biological diversity by setting aside large tracts of natural land.

1952

The nation elects Dwight D. Eisenhower its president. When he appoints two ex-car salesmen to his cabinet, including Douglas "Giveaway" McKay as Interior Secretary, defeated Democratic candidate, Adlai E. Stevenson, remarks: "The New Dealers have all left Washington to make way for the car dealers."

Aldo Leopold's notebook near his Wisconsin cabin. (Photo: Jim Brandenburg/Minden Pictures)

The majesty of a soaring great egret surely inspired the bird's adoption as the National Audubon Society's logo. (Photo: John Shaw)

Rush hour traffic on the Santa Monica Freeway in Los Angeles continues to grow since becoming an issue in the 1950s. (Photo: Gary Braasch)

The Empire State Building now uses its night lighting in celebratory fashion as well. (Photo: Esbin Anderson)

1953

The National Audubon Society again moves its headquarters, to Fifth Avenue and 94th Street. The Society also adopts a flying great egret (one of the chief victims of turn-of-the-century plume hunters) as its symbol.

1954

Supreme Court Justice, William O. Douglas, opposing a highway that would replace the Chesapeake and Ohio Canal, organizes a protest hike. Members of The Wilderness Society and National Audubon Society join Douglas on the 189-mile hike along the canal's tree-shaded towpath, and wide media coverage helps trash the plan. Audubon buys the last great stand of bald cypress in Florida's Corkscrew Swamp to establish the crown jewel of its sanctuary system.

1955

Conservationists build one of the most successful political coalitions of the era to fight the proposed Echo Park Dam in Utah's Dinosaur National Monument. This water-storage project would have flooded isolated canyons on the Green and Yampa rivers, but the five-year campaign prevents another loss akin to that of Hetch Hetchy.

1956

The Water Pollution Control Act is strengthened, providing money to build treatment plants. Marie Aull gives 70 acres in Dayton, Ohio, and the Aullwood Audubon Center and Farm is dedicated a year later. *Audubon* editor, John K. Terres, publicizes huge losses among migrant birds striking the Empire State Building. The building's management turns off the fixed-beam light atop the tower and installs rotating warning lights during migration.

1957

The Public Health Service, the federal agency charged with regulating water pollution, opens hearings on the wastes from packing plants along the Missouri River. Testimony describes blood, hooves, hair, and paunch manure from hundreds of thousands of slaughtered animals, mingled with raw domestic sewage, along a stretch of river tapped by over two million people for their drinking water.

1958

Stung by the launch of the first two manmade satellites in space by the Soviet Union (Sputnik I and II), the U.S. launches Explorer I and begins a nationwide drive to step up science education to help keep pace with Cold War foes.

1959

Queen Elizabeth II joins President Eisenhower in opening ceremonies for the St. Lawrence Seaway, which provides access from the Atlantic Ocean to the Great Lakes—alas, for invading pest organisms such as the zebra mussel, as well as for ships. Carl W. Buchheister succeeds John Baker as president of the National Audubon Society.

DECADE 1960–1969

1960

Charles H. Callison, a top environmental lobbyist in Washington, joins Audubon. He will focus on public land issues and help push through Congress the wilderness bill (which was finally passed in 1964). Alexander "Sandy" Sprunt, the Society's research director, heads its Continental Bald Eagle Project to chart the numbers, reproductive results, and sharp decline of that species as DDT spreads through ecosystems.

Dead fish and trash wash ashore. (Photo: M. Siluk)

A collection of homeowner pesticides. (Photo: Jack K. Clark)

The introduced zebra mussels (here on a clam shell) have become a threat to species native to the Great Lakes. (Photo: Robert Rattner)

Charles H. Callison joins the National Audubon Society in 1960 and singlehandedly lobbies for the enactment of landmark conservation legislation. (Photo courtesy the National Audubon Society)

1961

The pollution of shellfish beds around Raritan Bay is blamed for a hepatitis outbreak among 1,000 New Jersey residents. Among new conservation organizations founded this year are the World Wildlife Fund—U.S. and the Society of Tympanuchus Cupido Pinnatus Ltd., dedicated to the preservation of the prairie chicken.

1962

Rachel Carson's *Silent Spring* is published, and will become the all-time environmental classic. Congress amends the Bald Eagle Protection Act of 1940 to give similar protection to the golden eagle. Ironically, the impetus for the revision is that golden eagles look like the immatures of our national bird.

1963

A massive fish and wildlife kill occurs in the lower Mississippi River. "The bodies of turtles floated on the waters," *The New Republic* reports. "Tough 150-pound garfish and catfish weighing 70 pounds surfaced too weak to move. Crabs lay along the banks. Thousands of cranes and robins lay dead." Laboratory tests from some of the estimated five million dead fish implicate endrin, an insecticide related to DDT.

1964

Eight years of persuasion and invective, plus sixty-six versions of the bill, finally result in passage of the Wilderness Act. It amounts to a directive from Congress that federal agencies resist political pressure and save many large tracts of magnificent wild areas from cutting, mining, and other intrusions. The long campaign's "spiritual leader," Howard Zahniser of The Wilderness Society, dies three months before the bill's passage.

1965

Congress approves the Garrison Diversion Project, a colossal billion-dollar-plus boondoggle mandating 3,000 miles of canals, pipelines, drains, and reservoirs for the benefit of a few hundred North Dakota farmers. Taxpayers protest it will cost at least $700,000 for every beneficiary. Audubon will spend the rest of the century fighting the project in its various guises.

1966

Les Line becomes editor of *Audubon*, directing a makeover that will soon prompt *The New York Times* to call it "the most beautiful magazine in the world." With an extensive list of benefactors assembled in part by board members, and the magazine as a lure, membership soars from 36,000 in 1965 to 40,000 at the beginning of 1967, and to 60,000 only a year later.

1967

The Environmental Defense Fund is founded on New York's Long Island to stop the use of DDT. Audubon and EDF officials conspire during the Society's annual meeting to force Audubon's conservative board of directors to pass a resolution calling for a nationwide ban on the chemical. Carl Buchheister retires as president and Charles Callison is appointed Audubon's interim CEO.

1968

Elvis J. Stahr, Secretary of the Army in the Kennedy Administration and a former president of the University of Indiana, is named Audubon president. Stahr uses contacts in Congress and the Army Corps of Engineer to kill plans for a dam and reservoir in Kentucky's splendid Red River Gorge. Congress passes the National Wild and Scenic Rivers Act and the National Trails Act.

1969

Pressures on wildlife from residential developments, tapping scarce water supplies,

Senator Gaylord Nelson, founder of Earth Day and counselor to The Wilderness Society. (Photo courtesy of The Wilderness Society)

Right and below: Earth Day, 1970, protesters on the streets of New York City (right) and St. Louis. (photos: UPI/Corbis-Bettmann)

The bald eagle and its future generations are protected by Congressional legislation. (Photo: Art Wolfe)

and offroad traffic in dry regions of the West, prompt the founding of the Desert Fishes Council. Audubon, now one of the few leading conservation organizations with headquarters outside Washington, opens an office in the nation's capital.

DECADE 1970–1979

1970

Earth Day, the brainchild of Wisconsin's senator, Gaylord Nelson, is celebrated April 22 by 20 million Americans on campuses and in the streets all over the nation. President Richard M. Nixon establishes the Council on Environmental Quality, and Congress passes the National Environmental Policy Act (NEPA). Congress also passes a tough new Clean Air Act.

1971

The Murie Audubon Society in Casper, Wyoming, makes headlines across the country when members discover a graveyard of illegally poisoned eagles. In response, Congress tightens eagle protection legislation. The National Audubon Society moves to a great "glass box" on Manhattan's Third Avenue. New York's governor Nelson A. Rockefeller signs into law the Adirondack Park Agency Act, which for the first time gives a measure of protection to private lands as well as the "forever wild" forest within the park's boundaries.

1972

The campaign by the Environmental Defense Fund and the National Audubon Society ends in victory when the U.S. Environmental Protection Agency bans the discredited insecticide, DDT. Oregon passes the first bottle-recycling law. Stockholm, Sweden, hosts the first-of-its-kind United Nations Conference on the Human Environment.

1973

Congress passes the Endangered Species Act. Audubon biologist, Stephen W. Kress, starts an experimental project to return the Atlantic puffin, long ago extirpated from the area, to an island near the Audubon Camp of Maine.

1974

As the slaughter of the great whales continues, Audubon announces its first boycott, singling out products from the two largest whaling nations, Japan and the Soviet Union. The magazine is especially hard hit by the three-year boycott, losing lucrative ads for Japanese binoculars and cameras. The Worldwatch Institute is founded in Washington, D. C., to analyze emerging global problems and identify them for national leaders and the public.

1975

The winter roosts of blackbirds take a hit. Branding them as threats to human health, the U.S. Army announces plans to destroy the big nightly congregations of grackles, starlings, and redwings near military bases in Kentucky and Tennessee. Bird lovers protest the attacks, but the courts, and later Congress, uphold the Army's right to strike.

1976

Audubon president, Elvis Stahr, leads a successful drive to relax IRS restrictions on lobbying activities by nonprofit organizations. Now environmentalists can lobby legislators on comparatively even terms with their ideological adversaries. *Audubon* earns its first of two consecutive National Magazine Awards for Excellence in Reporting.

1977

Investigators determine that the Love Canal neighborhood at Niagara Falls, New York, is perched atop a large toxic waste dump, eventually prompting the evacuation of its residents. Across the continent, oil begins flowing southward through the Alaska pipeline from the North Slope to the port of Valdez.

Atlantic puffin on Machias Seal Island in Maine. (Photo: Arthur Morris/Birds As Art)

Red-winged blackbird perched on a branch in Tule Lake National Wildlife Refuge, California. (Photo: Darrell Gulin)

Elvis Stahr, president of the National Audubon Society during its period of greatest growth. (Photo courtesy the National Audubon Society)

A pond majestically presided over by the Alaska range in Denali National Park. (Photo: Carr Clifton/Minden Pictures)

1978

National Audubon continues its impressive growth through this environmental decade. As Elvis Stahr prepares to step down as president, he reports that in his ten-year tenure the Society grew from 88,000 to 388,000 members. During the same period, its net worth doubled to over $18.5 million, despite a surge in annual operating expenses from $2.5 million to $10.1 million. Protecting the environment has become big business.

1979

An accident at the Three Mile Island nuclear plant in Pennsylvania sours Americans on the once-heralded benefits of nuclear energy. Russell W. Peterson, a birdwatcher and former executive at DuPont, Governor of Delaware, and Chairman of the President's Council on Environmental Quality, succeeds Elvis Stahr as Audubon president.

DECADE 1980–1989

1980

Swayed by a well-orchestrated campaign carried out by the nation's leading conservation organizations, Congress passes the Alaska National Interest Lands Conservation Act. In one swoop, the act adds more than 100 million acres to the federal wildlands system. On a somber note, National Audubon joins the Fish and Wildlife Service in a last-ditch effort to save the California condor from extinction.

1981

As Ronald Reagan starts his first term as U.S. president, the environmental community braces for an assault on recent hard-won gains. Interior Secretary, James Watt, leads the charge, skirting wildlife protection and anti-pollution laws to push for increased oil drilling, logging, and mining on public lands.

1982

As some California environmentalists attack the aggressive condor management techniques planned by Audubon and federal biologists, Audubon leader, Russ Peterson, meets with state wildlife officials to gain concessions. The agreement permits biologists to trap condors for radio tracking and captive-breeding programs.

1983

Meetings at the White House between conservation leaders and President Reagan's aides fail to bring changes in the administration's hard-line stand on environmental policies. Eleven of the top sixteen places in Watt's Interior Department are filled by ex-officials in the the five major industries (including oil, forestry, and ranching) regulated by the agency.

1984

With Ted Turner's help, Russ Peterson launches *The World of Audubon* TV series. Hollywood stars such as Robert Redford, Meryl Streep, and Cliff Robertson narrate the programs. With Audubon Junior Clubs long dormant, the Society moves back into children's education with a popular new program and publication, *Audubon Adventures*.

1985

French agents sink the Greenpeace vessel *Rainbow Warrior*, which was planning to disrupt nuclear tests in the South Pacific. Congress enacts the Conservation Reserve Program to combat erosion and preserve cover for nesting waterfowl. Peter A.A. Berle, former chief of the New York State Department of Environmental Conservation, succeeds Peterson as Audubon president.

Massive clearcutting in Olympic National Park, Washington. (Photo: Gary Braasch)

Oil washed onto the shore of Knights Island from the Exxon Valdez *tanker spill. (Photo: Gary Braasch)*

Sandhill cranes on the Platte River in Nebraska. (Photo: Tom Mangelsen)

1986

Because of dioxin contamination, the U.S. Environmental Protection Agency evacuates residents from Times Beach, Missouri, and buys the whole town.

1987

The last wild California condor, AC 9, is captured by Audubon biologists and put into a captive-breeding program with other survivors. An uprising among Audubon activists, led by former Audubon VP Charles Callison, is a response to the board's plans to close regional offices and cut the chapters' share of dues. The board conciliates and makes room for nine members to be elected by the chapters.

1988

The first condor chick is born in captivity in California, raising new hope for the species' survival.

1989

The supertanker *Exxon Valdez* blunders onto rocks in Alaska's Prince William Sound. Despite an enormous effort at containment by government workers and volunteers, the worst oil spill in maritime history kills 50,000 birds and countless other animals and plants.

DECADE 1990–1998

1990

Protection of the Platte River, one of Audubon's top campaign priorities, wins big: the EPA vetoes construction of the proposed Two Forks Dam near Denver on the South Platte. The dam would have destroyed critical stretches where half a million sandhill cranes (80 percent of the world's population) stop during their migrations.

1991

The addition of Oregon's Tenmile Creek Audubon Sanctuary preserves a key piece of the largest unlogged coastal temperate rainforest left in the U.S. A prominent resident there is the marbled murrelet, a threatened and aberrant seabird that nests in trees. Michael Robbins becomes editor of *Audubon*.

1992

Audubon president, Peter Berle, becomes the first American to testify before a committee of the new Russian parliament, advocating an international park overarching Alaska and the Russian Far East. The Society moves into its new home at 700 Broadway in Manhattan—one of the most environmentally advanced, energy-efficient office buildings in the world.

1993

Audubon acquires 76 acres of private holdings in California's Bitter Creek National Wildlife Refuge and turns it over to the Fish and Wildlife Service for its pending release into the wild of captive condors. More than 600,000 children are enrolled in the *Audubon Adventures* program.

1994

The bald eagle, a victim of DDT but a beneficiary of the Endangered Species Act, is down-listed from the "endangered" category to "threatened." After a grueling fifteen-year campaign led by Audubon and the Mono Lake Committee, California's Water Board halts the diversion of water to Los Angeles from Mono Lake in the Eastern Sierra. The decision restores adequate water levels at this lake, which is vital to western aquatic birds.

1995

John Flicker succeeds Peter Berle as Audubon president. The gray wolf is introduced by federal biologists into the Yellowstone ecosystem and wilderness areas of Idaho. Under the cloak of their "Contract With America," right-wingers in Congress take aim at environmental laws: a rider, dubbed "Logging Without Laws," slips through in a budget bill. But another budget bill, containing a rider opening the Arctic National Wildlife Refuge to oil drilling, is vetoed by President Clinton.

Marbled murrelet drawing by John James Audubon. (Courtesy the National Audubon Society)

Snow-covered tufa towers in Mono Lake, California. (Photo: Kathleen Norris Cook)

Bison cow and calf on the plains of Montana. (Photo: Daniel J. Cox/Natural Exposures)

1996

The Society begins to put into effect its "Strategic Plan for Audubon 2000." The plan reasserts Audubon's commitment to protecting birds, other wildlife, and their habitat. It also moves to decentralize the organization, opening new state offices and building an effective grassroots network. The magazine's series "What Good Is An Ecosystem?" emphasizes the importance of deserts, forests, wetlands, and prairies.

1997

Audubon lobbyists help beat back attempts in Congress to weaken the Endangered Species Act. They also derail the $1.4 billion resurrection of the Garrison Diversion Project in North Dakota. Writer Doug Peacock's "The Yellowstone Massacre" in *Audubon* draws national attention to the killing of bison in the national park.

1998

House Speaker Newt Gingrich and fellow Republicans announce plans for a multimillion-dollar cleanup of California's Salton Sea as a memorial to the late entertainer Sonny Bono, who was the area's representative in Congress. Lisa Gosselin becomes editor of *Audubon*. Audubon holds its first-ever Great Backyard Bird Count; 14,000 individuals, classrooms, and families across the country identify, count, and report the birds they see in their backyards, schoolyards, and parks.

ACKNOWLEDGEMENTS

Les Line would like to thank writers Frank Graham Jr., George Laycock, Jon Luoma, John Mitchell, Peter Steinhart, and Ted Williams, and picture editor Niki Barrie for the pleasure of working with them once again; Katherine Santone and Hugh Lauter Levin for providing the opportunity; and Jim Muschett for keeping the project on track. He also wishes to remember the former chief executives of the National Audubon Society who supported the editorial independence of *Audubon* magazine—Carl Buchheister, Charles Callison, Elvis Stahr, and Russell Peterson—and the NAS staff members, grass-roots activists, and directors who helped define the Audubon Cause.

Audubon Books wishes to thank Gray Coleman for the introduction; Hugh Levin and Jim Muschett for the pleasure of working with two consummate professionals; *Audubon* magazine's editorial staff for their invaluable help; John Bianchi for his discerning comments; and our president, John Flicker, for a vision that will shepherd the National Audubon Society into its second century of conservation.

In addition to the above, Levin Associates wishes to thank Katherine Santone and the staff of Audubon books, and the many organizations and individuals who have contributed generously to this book.

A group of fledgling chickadees line up on a tree branch. (Photo: Art Wolfe)

A pair of reddish egrets perform their mating dance on Sanibel Island, Florida. (Photo: Art Morris/Birds As Art)